Ojai Valley Make-Ahead Cookbook

vegetarian recipes and tips
to make serving dinner effortless

By Randy Graham

© September 1, 2018
Randolph B. Graham
All Rights Reserved

Ojai, California

Front cover photo: Randy Graham

Other books in this series:
Ojai Valley Slow Cooker Cookbook
Ojai Valley Gluten-Free Cookbook
Ojai Valley Vegetarian Cookbook
Ojai Valley Grill It Cookbook
Ojai Valley Vegan Cookbook

Many thanks to my friends for reviewing my draft and providing input prior to submitting this book for publication: Stacey Jones, Tom & Cathy Okerlund, Teresa Smith, Cheryl Mankin, Linda Knight, Jessie Austin, Jeni Short, Carol Miller, Melani Jean, Andrea Neal, Marcia Morris, Valerie Gebroe, Diane Farnham, Vicki Means, Lisa Meeker, Robin Pagliasotti, Sylvia Garcia, Nani Lawrence, Breena Maggio, Leslie McCleary, Carla Mezori, and Star Maynes.

Table of Contents

Introduction

The Benefits of Make-Ahead Meals

Meal Planning Tips

Tips for Storing and Reheating

Freezer Recipes
1. Meaty Nut Loaf
2. Three Cheese Lasagna
3. Brown Rice & Black Bean Casserole
4. Eggplant Parmigiano-Reggiano
5. Chik'n Enchiladas *VEGAN*
6. Hearty Cannellini Bean Casserole *VEGAN*
7. Hearty Kale & Sausage Turnovers
8. Hearty Quinoa Burger
9. Jollof Rice Bowl
10. Lemony Artichoke Turnovers
11. Malt Ball Cupcakes
12. Marinara Sauce *VEGAN*
13. Black Beans, Chard and Sorghum Bowl
14. Oatmeal Bread
15. Orzo Pasta with Asiago Cheese
16. Quinoa and Chik'n Casserole *VEGAN*
17. Tempeh Salisbury Steak
18. Bread Pudding
19. Vegetarian Jambalaya
20. Veggie Meatballs

Refrigerator Recipes

21 Asparagus and Gruyère Quiche
22 Back-to-Our Root Vegetables
23 Burrata Lasagna
24 Cabbage and Chickpea Soup *VEGAN*
25 Chana Masala *VEGAN*
26 Cheesy-Creamy Cauliflower
27 Chickpea Veggie Patty Burger
28 Collard Greens with Veggie Sausage
29 Creamy Vodka Sauce
30 Earthy Mushroom & Gruyère Quiche
31 Gran's Carrot Casserole
32 Hearty Chili Bean Soup *VEGAN*
33 Hearty Ratatouille *VEGAN*
34 Jalapeño Cheese Bread
35 Idaho Potatoes
36 Jalapeño Corn Chowder
37 Jim's Mom's Southern Candied Yams
38 Kale-Wakame Soup *VEGAN*
39 Kohlrabi Soup
40 Mac 'N' Cheese with Smoked Gouda
41 Matzo Ball Soup
42 Mushroom Goulash *VEGAN*
43 Portobello Wellington Appetizers
44 Roasted Red Pepper and Carrot Soup *VEGAN*
45 Robin's Tortilla Soup
46 Spicy Cauliflower Garbanzo Coconut Stew
47 Tabouli Salad
48 Tahini-Herb Dip *VEGAN*
49 Chèvre Cheese Pasta - Mac & Cheese Style
50 Tarragon Salad Dressing *VEGAN*
51 Robin's Three Bean Salad *VEGAN*
52 Forbidden Rice Salad *VEGAN*

Index of Recipes by Title

Index of Ingredients by Recipe

About the Author

Additional Ojai Valley Cookbooks

Introduction

Are you looking for a cookbook that features easy-to-make meals that can be either refrigerated for the next day or frozen for use later in the week? If yes, then this book is for you.

The recipes are divided into two categories: freezer recipes and refrigerator recipes. What's the difference? The freezer recipes hold up well for many weeks in the freezer. By this, I mean the *texture* holds up well after unthawing and reheating. The refrigerator recipes do not hold up as well. These are best to make-ahead, refrigerate, and serve the next day.

The 52 recipes in this book are 100% vegetarian. In addition, 14 of the recipes are also vegan and are denoted as such in the table of contents. All recipes are my own creation and/or adaptions from other recipes I have admired and served over the last 40 years.

See my Meaty Nut Loaf (1) freezer recipe. I have served this for 37 years at Thanksgiving and Christmas to the enjoyment of my family and visiting omnivore friends. The next day I like to cut a ¾-inch slice off the leftover loaf and make sandwiches.

You will also like my Chana Masala (25) refrigerator recipe. This vegan and gluten-free recipe is a savory dish of cooked garbanzo beans (chickpeas), onion, garlic, bay leaves and various Indian spices. It gets its heat from small red chiles and although I use one chile only when I make it, you can add more if you like it hotter.

Some of my recipes, including Back-to-Our Root Vegetables (22), specify organic ingredients. If you can't find or can't afford organic, it's OK to use non-organic ingredients. The recipes work well either way, but I encourage you to buy fresh, local, and organic whenever you can.

My hope is that you will enjoy these recipes as much as my friends and family have enjoyed them. May you eat well, eat local, and eat fresh!

The Benefits of Make-Ahead Meals

The major benefit of make-ahead-meals is that they are nutritious and taste wonderful when reheated. Here are some of the other benefits.

>**Quick**: Imagine that it is that time of day when the kids are suddenly restless, agitated, and whiney (which usually hits right about the time you need to be getting dinner on the table). So, there you are with a toddler on your hip, trying to make dinner with one hand, begging your 5-year old not to tease the cat. You can avoid these, and other dinnertime headaches, by quickly reheating frozen or refrigerated meals.

>**Healthy:** When you have healthy, make-ahead meals waiting for you at home, you are less likely to find yourself in the drive-through at Micky D's picking up fast food on your way home from work. Many commercially prepared foods are high in fat, salt, and sugar. When we prepare our own food, we know exactly which ingredients and how much of each are going into our food.

>**Convenient:** When you plan your meals for the next week, you can cook when you want to cook (as opposed to cooking on demand). You can go shopping for ingredients when you want to shop (as opposed to that last minute trip to the store to get that one important ingredient without which the meal can't be made).

I recommend setting time aside on a Saturday morning to plan, to shop, and to make many of the next week's meals all at once. Then refrigerate or freeze them to be reheated as needed.

Cost: Eating homemade meals is usually much cheaper than eating at a restaurant, or buying processed foods from the market. When we eat at a restaurant, we pay for not only the food, but also the costs of running that business (lights, water, electricity, gas, the building, and the staff). The same goes for the pre-made or frozen meals at grocery stores.

Leftovers: If you have unexpected leftover food after dinner, refrigerate or freeze it for reheating another day. For example, make my Meaty Nutloaf (1) ahead of time and enjoy it for dinner on Tuesday, then use the leftovers in meatloaf sandwiches for Wednesday lunch. Kind of a "twofer" make-ahead!

Variety: If you are able to put thought into your meals ahead of time, it will become easy to choose from several different food categories (protein, fat, grains, vegetables, etc.) in order to get the variety you and your family need. As you plan ahead, feel free to mix it up every week. You won't be limited to the basic foods you make out of habit because meal prep encourages you to get more creative by looking up new recipes. The recipes in this book will give you a head start!

One last thought: There is no right or wrong way to achieve a meal prep routine. Everyone has their own way of doing it. Know that it may take some trial and error before it becomes routine.

Meal Planning Tips

Meal planning is a vital part of eating a healthy diet. I highly encourage you to take half an hour a week to plan healthy meals for your family the next week. It will take a little up front time to plan for the entire week, but your time will be well worth it. Here's an example of what to plan and what to make for dinner for the first week. This will also help when you make your list of ingredients needed for the entire week.

>**Monday:** Earthy Mushroom and Gruyère Quiche (30) as a refrigerator entrée. Serve with a bowl of Lindsay "smooth and buttery" green ripe olives. Add a salad of your choice if you have the energy. I recommend a simple green salad made with chopped head lettuce and my Tarragon Salad Dressing (50). And to start the week off on a festive note, I recommend unthawing my Malt Ball Cupcakes (11) for dessert. If you make enough, there will be leftover cupcakes for lunches or for a mid-afternoon snack for the kids after school (OK...not as healthy as carrot sticks and apple slices after school...but what the heck).

>**Tuesday:** Hearty Chili Bean Soup (32) as a refrigerator entrée. Add unthawed Jalapeño Cheese Bread (34) from the freezer and you have a lip-smacking-good and nutritious meal. Easy-peasy.

Wednesday: Consider making meals for Wednesday nights from leftovers from the previous two or three days. For example, if there are leftovers from Monday and Tuesday, reheat them and add rice or a fresh green salad (or both) to the plate.

Thursday: Mac 'N' Cheese with Smoked Gouda (40) as a refrigerator entrée. Serve with fresh sliced tomatoes as a side dish.

Friday: Hearty Quinoa Burger (8) as the entrée from the freezer. Reheat and serve with fresh hamburger buns, lettuce, sliced onions, sliced tomatoes, and secret sauce. I like to eat these with potato chips. Even your teenagers will stick around to eat this dinner!

Saturday: Meaty Nut Loaf (1) as the entrée from the freezer. Add Idaho Potatoes (35) from the refrigerator as well as Robin's Three Bean Salad (51). Nuff said. Comfort food for sure.

Sunday: After a wonderful day with the family, pull out my Eggplant Parmigiano-Reggiano (4) from the freezer and reheat as directed. Add a fresh baguette and a simple salad and you have a complete meal. As you go to sleep that night, be sure to thank yourself for making the effort to plan ahead. We all deserve a self-congratulatory pat on the back once in a while.

Tips for Storing and Reheating

Plastic: Look for the Resin Identification Code (RIC) on the bottom of each plastic container. These codes indicate what type of plastic is being used in that container.

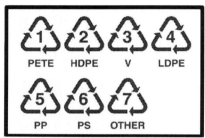

[source: simplyorganicbeauty.com]

If you see the number 1, this indicates the plastic is polyethylene terephthalate. Although the Food and Drug Administration (FDA) considers it safe for the storage of many food products (particularly bottled water or carbonated soft drinks), safety when used for freezing and reheating of foods is undetermined.

If you see the number 6 on containers it is made with polystyrene; popularly known as Styrofoam. Not safe for freezing or reheating.

If you see triangles with the numbers 3 or 7, that container might release chemicals like BPA (bisphenol A) or PVC (phthalates). Also not safe.

If these plastic storage containers are not safe (or at best "generally considered" to be safe) why take chances with your health by using them? The numbers 2, 4, or 5 are generally considered safe for food and/or drinks. My recommendation is to use these for short-term storage of food in the refrigerator. Plastic wrap that is BPA-free is OK for short periods of storage in the refrigerator or freezer (see my Jalapeño Cheese Bread (35) recipe).

Glass: The use of tempered glass containers for hot or cold food storage in either the refrigerator or freezer is your best bet. They are more expensive than plastic but provide important safety benefits.

Here is a list of the top 10 reasons why you should consider using glass containers [source: topratedkitchen.com].

- Glass in food storage has a zero rate of chemical interaction, is nonporous and impermeable so there is nothing to affect the consistency, aroma, or flavor of your stored food. It also aids in minimizing refrigerator odors.

- Food simply tastes better when reheated in glass, whether in a conventional oven or microwave...food does not seem to hold its full flavor when nuked in plastic!

- Most glass storage containers are made from oven-proof, freezer-safe and dishwasher-safe tempered glass. You can move stored foods between freezer to stove, oven or microwave, and then to refrigerator without the fear of cracked, broken, or shattered glass.

- Glass bases are both top and bottom-rack dishwasher safe without the concern for high heat sanitizing settings or abrasive dishwasher detergents.

- Clear glass food storage containers make it much easier to see what you've stored, especially when using them in a refrigerator or freezer where things often get pushed to the back and forgotten.

- You can place hot food in a glass food storage container immediately after cooking without having to wait for it to cool down. This means the kitchen dishes get done faster.

- Glass storage containers, unless they get broken, last many years, saving you all the money you would otherwise spend replacing stained and blistered plastic containers. While costing a little more up front, they pay big dividends over time.

- If you should break a glass food container by accident, know that up to 80 percent of discarded glass can be recycled. The glass recycling process uses 40 percent less energy than manufacturing new glass and will provide the same quality, characteristics and performance as new.

- Glass is, overall, a safer bet for food storage than plastic. Though polycarbonate plastic is strong and long-lasting, it can break down over time from high temperatures and overuse.

- Using glass is environmentally responsible, reducing the amount of plastic in our landfills. When you invest in glass storage containers, you eliminate the mismatched mess of plastic containers in your kitchen cabinets or pantry with something that looks great, is very versatile in its uses, and lasts a really long time.

Borosilicate Glass: If you freeze and unthaw most of your meals, you might consider Borosilicate glass containers because they are resistant to thermal shock. Know, however, that they are more brittle than tempered glass containers and more expensive.

Storing: If using plastic containers, cover and refrigerate or freeze each meal soon after it cools. If using glass, you need to be careful not to put hot containers on a wet or cold surface. They should cool on a rack or on a piece of dry cloth before covering and refrigerating or freezing.

Thawing: Know that freezing food puts disease-causing bacteria in suspended animation but does not kill them. As soon as food gets warmer (temperatures above 40 degrees Fahrenheit) bacteria will begin to multiply. So, when thawing frozen food, it's important to keep it out of the "danger zone" of temperatures where bacteria thrive. Here are three methods that I've used for safely thawing out frozen foods:

- Refrigerator: This is the easiest method but it takes a long time, so you must plan ahead. You may want to thaw a dinner entree in the refrigerator during the day while you're at work. The advantages to this method are that it's hands-off and the refrigerator keeps food at a safe temperature.

- Cold Water: Sealed packages of food may be thawed in cold water. Place the package under water in a bowl, pot, or sink and change the water every 30 minutes until the food is defrosted.

- Room Temperature: Breads are best if thawed for 2 to 4 hours at room temperature. Do not use this method for vegetables.

Reheating: The best way to reheat anything is in a toaster oven (if you have one). Plus, it is way more convenient than a normal oven if you are reheating food for one person. Make sure that freezer meals are totally thawed before using the oven, then 10 to 15 minutes at 350 degrees should do the trick.

The best method for reheating thawed out casseroles is in a conventional oven. If reheating my Orzo Pasta with Asiago Cheese (16) or my Chik'n Enchiladas (6), for example, place them (uncovered) in the oven, set the heat to 350 degrees, and heat for approximately 15 minutes or until heated through.

To reheat meals on top of the stove, such as my Cabbage and Chickpea Soup (25) or my Jalapeño Corn Chowder (37), place them in a large saucepan (or soup pot) on medium heat for about 10 minutes or until the soup begins to bubble around the edges.

The microwave should be your last resort. If you *have* to use it for anything other than soups or chowders, use the reheat setting and put a half-filled cup of water next to the food to help keep it moist. I know that sounds weird, but it works.

Freezer Recipes

[Eggplant Parmigiano-Reggiano]

1 Meaty Nutloaf

Nut loaf recipes became popular in the United States, during World War I, when meat was scarce. They became popular, again, when food was rationed during World War II. How can you make a vegetarian dish that is 'meaty'? Oxymoron you say? Try it. I think you'll be surprised.

This is a recipe I have served over the last 37 years at Thanksgiving and Christmas to the enjoyment of my family and visiting omnivore friends. The next day I like to cut a ¾ inch slice off the leftover loaf and make sandwiches.

Ingredients:
1½ cups walnuts
½ cup unsalted cashews or almonds
2 tablespoons unsalted butter
1 yellow onion (chopped fine)
2 teaspoons minced garlic
1½ cup cooked brown rice (white is OK but brown is tastier)
2 tablespoons parsley (chopped)
1 tablespoon fresh marjoram (chopped)
2 tablespoons fresh thyme (chopped)
1 teaspoon fresh sage leaves (chopped)
4 eggs (lightly beaten)
8 ounces Gruyère cheese (grated)
1 cup cottage cheese
1 teaspoon salt
½ teaspoon freshly ground black pepper

Directions:

Grease a 9-inch loaf pan (you can use shortening or cooking oil). A round 9-inch spring form pan works well also. Set aside.

Toast walnuts and cashews on a baking sheet until lightly browned, about ten minutes. Do not burn. Let cool. Finely chop and set aside (I use a blender to chop the nuts). Increase oven temperature to 375 degrees.

Melt butter in a saucepan over medium heat. Add onion and garlic. Cook until translucent, about three minutes. Transfer to a large bowl and add toasted nuts, rice, parsley, marjoram, thyme, sage, eggs, Gruyère, cottage cheese, salt, and pepper. Mix well. Pour mixture into prepared pan, cover, and freeze.

To serve, unthaw loaf completely. Bake at 350 until golden brown and firm to the touch, about 50 to 55 minutes. Serve with potatoes, gravy, and your favorite side dishes.

2   Three Cheese Lasagna

I was going to call this recipe Three-Cheese, Three-Layer Lasagna with Burnt Marinara. *What?* you might ask. Let me explain.

Robin makes a wonderful marinara sauce that takes a couple of hours to reduce down and is amazing. Is it burnt? Kinda-sorta. Maybe. I prefer to say it is slow-roasted on the stovetop. This is something her mother taught her to do many moons ago. I'd never had anything like it until she made it for me 35 years ago. It is the perfect sauce for my three-cheese lasagna.

Now, something about three cheeses and three layers. You may have seen recipes for lasagna with Parmesan, mozzarella and ricotta cheeses. I use an aged Parmigiano-Reggiano instead of the finely grated parmesan packaged in the grocery store's grab-and-go tub. I also like Provolone because its flavor and texture are the perfect complement to the Parmigiano-Reggiano and mozzarella cheeses.

If you can't find or don't want to use a nice, aged Parmigiano-Reggiano cheese, use whatever parmesan you like. But try it, at least this once, with a good quality Parmigiano-Reggiano. It makes a big difference in taste.

This recipe makes a bunch of lasagna, but not to worry. If you and your tribe don't polish it all off in one sitting, it is just as tasty when reheated the next day. Or cut it into serving sizes that suit you and your family, freeze, and bring it out for dinner a week or two later. They'll wonder why you didn't bring it out sooner!

Ingredients:
3 tablespoons extra-virgin olive oil
1 cup onion (chopped fine)
4 cloves garlic (peeled and minced)
6 ounces tomato paste
2 26-ounce boxes Pomi strained tomatoes
12 lasagna noodles (cook according to package directions)
6 ounces fresh baby spinach
6 ounces sun dried tomato strips (not in oil)
9 slices mozzarella cheese
9 slices Provolone cheese
2 cups grated Parmigiano-Reggiano cheese (grated fine)
Salt and pepper to taste

Directions:
Preheat oven to 375 degrees. Coat a 9x13-inch baking pan with cooking spray.

To make the sauce, heat the olive oil in a large saucepan on medium heat. Add the onions and sauté for five minutes. Add garlic, stir, and cook for another three minutes. Add tomato paste and stir to combine. Cook this thick onion/garlic/tomato paste for about five minutes while stirring occasionally. Add Pomi, stir to combine and reduce heat to low. Cover and simmer for 45 to 50 minutes, stirring occasionally. Uncover, remove from heat and set aside.

While the sauce is simmering, prepare the noodles. Bring a large pot of water (add a pinch of salt) to boil and cook the noodles according to package directions. Remove the noodles from the water and lay out on a clean towel. Cover with another towel and set aside.

Assembly:
Spread 1/3 cup of the sauce on the bottom of the prepared baking pan. Layer three of the noodles over the sauce (trim to fit the length of the pan if necessary). Spread another 1/3 cup sauce on top of the noodles. Make a layer of spinach on top and layer the sundried tomatoes on top of that. Layer the nine slices of mozzarella on top. This completes the first layer.

Create the second layer by layering three noodles on top of the first layer. Spread another 1/3 cup sauce on top of the noodles. Make a layer of spinach on top and layer the nine slices of Provolone on top of that. This completes the second layer.

Create the third layer using another 3 noodles. Spread another 1/3 cup sauce on top of the noodles. Make a layer of spinach on top and sprinkle the Parmigiano-Reggiano cheese on top of that. Layer with the last three noodles and spread another 1/3 cup sauce on top. This completes the layers. Cover and freeze.

To serve, unthaw and bake, covered, for 45 minutes. Remove cover, and bake for another 15 minutes. Remove from the oven and allow to cool for approximately 5 minutes before serving.

3 Brown Rice and Black Bean Casserole

This is a hearty, nutritious casserole dish. I've even enjoyed serving it as a hot dip along with corn chips. The professor in my nutrition class at Berkeley would have said that this is a "good news" recipe because it's a good example of combining legumes (beans), grain (rice) and dairy (cheese) for complete protein. The even better news? It's tasty. Very tasty!

Ingredients:
1 tablespoon olive oil
1/3 cup onion (diced)
1 medium zucchini (thinly sliced)
½ cup mushrooms (sliced)
½ teaspoon cumin
½ teaspoon salt
Fresh ground pepper to taste
1 cup cooked brown rice
15-ounce can black beans (drained)
4-ounce can diced green chiles (drained)
1 Jalapeño or Serrano chile (seeded and diced)
1/3 cup shredded carrots
2 cups shredded Swiss cheese (Gruyère works well too)

Directions:
Prepare a 9x9-inch baking dish with cooking spray.

Heat the olive oil in a skillet over medium heat, add onion and cook until the onion is just tender. Mix in the zucchini and mushrooms. Season with cumin, salt, and pepper. Cook, stirring occasionally, until zucchini is lightly browned.

In large bowl, mix the onion/zucchini/mushroom mixture with the cooked rice, beans, chiles, carrots, and half of the cheese. Transfer to prepared baking dish. Sprinkle top with remaining cheese.

Cover casserole loosely with foil making sure the foil does not touch the top with the cheese. Freeze.

To serve, unthaw casserole completely.

Bake for 30 minutes at 350 degrees. Uncover, and continue baking 10 minutes more, or until bubbly and lightly browned. Serve with a fresh garden salad and a full-bodied red wine for a complete, nutritious meal.

4   Eggplant Parmigiano-Reggiano

When I served this eggplant dish the other night our friends asked, "What's the difference between Parmesan and Parmigiano-Reggiano cheese?" I replied by saying, "Well, they're kinda the same thing but different."

Looking perplexed, Lol asked, "How can they be the same thing yet different?" It's no wonder that he's a successful trial attorney. This is what I told our dinner guests while they ate with *gusto*.

Parmigiano is an alternative and more authentic spelling for Parmesan but it is more than that. Parmigiano refers to the province of Parma where the production of Parmigiano cheeses is strictly controlled by Italian law.

In 1934, cheese producers in both the Parma and Reggio-Emilia provinces joined forces with producers in the Modena and Mantua provinces to form an association called the Consorzio del Grana Tipico. Cheese producers from the province of Bologna later joined the group. In 1954, they renamed their group the *Consorzio del Formaggio Parmigiano-Reggiano.* Hence the name Parmigiano-Reggiano.

My eggplant recipe features properly cooked, but not squishy, rounds of eggplant with a crisp crust, authentic Italian Parmigiano-Reggiano cheese, and an aromatic tomato sauce. It is melt-in-your-mouth good. No more need be said.

Ingredients:
3 medium eggplants (cut crosswise into ¼-inch-thick rounds)
3¼ teaspoons salt
3 pounds fresh plum tomatoes
1½ cups plus 3 tablespoons olive oil
2 large garlic cloves (chopped fine)
20 fresh basil leaves (tear in half)
¾ teaspoon fresh ground black pepper
¼ teaspoon crushed red pepper flakes
1 cup flour
5 large eggs
3½ cups Italian breadcrumbs
2/3 cup Parmigiano-Reggiano cheese (finely grated)
16 ounces whole milk mozzarella (thinly sliced)

Directions:
Toss eggplant with two teaspoons salt in a colander set over a bowl. Let it drain out excess moisture – about 30 minutes.

While eggplant drains, cut a small "X" in bottom of each tomato with a sharp paring knife and blanch them in a 5-quart pot of boiling water for one minute. Make sure the water is boiling before adding tomatoes. Using a slotted spoon, transfer tomatoes to a cutting board and, when cool enough to handle, peel off skin beginning from scored end. Coarsely chop tomatoes, then purée in batches in a blender.

Heat 3 tablespoons of the oil in a 5-quart heavy pot over moderately high heat until hot but not smoking. Add garlic and sauté, stirring, until golden, about 30 seconds. Add tomato purée, basil, 1 teaspoon salt, ½ teaspoon pepper, and red pepper flakes. Simmer uncovered, stirring occasionally, until slightly thickened – about 25 to 30 minutes. Set aside.

Stir together flour, remaining ¼ teaspoon salt, and remaining ¼ teaspoon pepper in a shallow bowl. Lightly beat eggs in a second shallow bowl. In a third shallow bowl, stir together breadcrumbs and 1/3 cup Parmesan. Set all three aside.

Gently wipe each eggplant slice with a paper towel to remove excess moisture and salt. Working with one slice at a time, dredge eggplant in flour, then dip in egg, letting excess drip off, and dredge in breadcrumbs until evenly coated. Transfer eggplant to sheets of wax paper, arranging slices in a single layer. Heat remaining 1½ cups oil in a deep skillet over moderately high heat and fry eggplant for three to four minutes per side. Transfer with tongs to paper towels to drain. Set aside.

Spread 1 cup tomato sauce in bottom of a rectangular (9x13x2-inch) baking dish. Arrange one third of eggplant slices in one layer over sauce, overlapping slightly. Cover eggplant with one third of remaining sauce and one third of mozzarella. Continue layering with remaining eggplant, sauce, and mozzarella. Sprinkle top with remaining 1/3 cup Parmesan. Cover and freeze.

To serve, unthaw and bake, uncovered, at 375 degrees until cheese is melted and golden and sauce is bubbling - about 35 to 40 minutes. Serve with a fresh garden salad and fresh-baked French bread hot from the oven.

5   Chik'n Enchiladas _VEGAN_

This is an easy and flavorful vegan enchilada dish. The combination of sautéed spinach, onions, and sweet corn is unusual and when paired with my Azteca sauce it makes a hearty, nutritious, and fun entrée. Serve with rice and warm tortillas of your choice for a complete dinner.

Enchilada Ingredients:
1 tablespoon olive oil
½ onion (fine chop)
14 ounces fresh baby spinach
1 cup sweet cut corn
Azteca sauce (see recipe below)
15 corn tortillas (cut in half)
1 cup black beans (rinsed)
2 cups Quorn Chik'n Tenders (each tender cut in half)
2 green onions (chopped for garnish)

Enchilada Directions:
Heat oil in a large frying pan over medium heat. Add onion and cook until translucent, about 4 minutes. Add spinach and cook, stirring as needed, until almost completely wilted. Add corn and cook until hot. Set aside.

Using a 9x13 inch baking dish, spreading one-third of the sauce over the bottom, top with one-third of the tortillas (slightly overlapped) and all of the beans and Chik'n tenders. Top with one-third of tortillas, one third of the sauce, and all of the vegetable mixture. Complete the enchiladas with the remaining tortillas and remaining sauce. Cover and freeze.

To serve, unthaw completely. Set oven to 375 degrees and bake until bubbling and tortillas are starting to brown on edges - about 30 minutes. Sprinkle with green onions prior to serving.

Azteca Sauce Ingredients:
1 small white onion (fine dice)
½ tablespoon olive oil
1 clove garlic (minced)
28-ounce can crushed tomatoes (do not drain)
1 cup hot water
1 teaspoon Better Than Bouillon Vegetable Base
½ teaspoon salt
1 tablespoon red chili powder
¼ cup chopped cilantro

Azteca Sauce Directions:
Heat the oil in a frying pan over medium heat. Add onion and cook until translucent (about five minutes). Add garlic and cook for another minute or two. Add crushed tomatoes, water, Better Than Bouillon, salt, and chili powder. Stir till well mixed. Simmer uncovered over low heat for approximately 15 to 20 minutes until sauce begins to thicken. Stir in cilantro, remove from heat, and set aside.

6 Hearty Cannellini Bean Casserole *VEGAN*

Cannellini beans are a large white variety of kidney bean. They are popular in Central and Southern Italy. You may recognize them as the classic bean found in minestrone soup.

I use cannellini in this hearty casserole for a couple of reasons. Using cannellini beans gives the dish superior texture plus the beans get the chance to soak up all the flavors of the garlic and herbs.

Once you read through the recipe one time, you'll see that this is not a difficult dish to make. It is time consuming, but your efforts will be rewarded with unmatched freshness and taste from stove to freezer to table!

Ingredients:
2 14-ounce cans cannellini beans
6 sprigs plus 1½ tablespoons chopped fresh thyme (divided)
3 sprigs plus 3 tablespoons chopped parsley (divided)
½ medium white onion (peeled but not diced)
3 whole cloves garlic
1 medium fennel bulb (stalks and fronds reserved; bulb quartered and diced)
12 cloves garlic (6 cloves peeled and halved; 6 cloves minced)
3 tablespoons olive oil (divided)
2 cups carrots (diced)
1 large white onion (diced)
1 teaspoon white wine vinegar

1½ cups reserved liquid
1½ cups fresh breadcrumbs

Directions:
Put beans and liquid in a 5½ to 6-quart Dutch oven (I use an All-Clad stainless steel Dutch oven) and add enough water to cover by two inches. Tie six thyme sprigs and three parsley sprigs together and add to pot. Pierce onion half with cloves and add to pot. Add fennel fronds and stalks (but not the bulb) to pot with the six halved garlic cloves.

Partially cover, and bring to a boil. Uncover, reduce heat to medium-low, and simmer 35 to 40 minutes, or until beans are just tender. Drain beans, and reserve cooking liquid. Set both the beans and reserved cooking liquid aside in separate bowls. Discard herb bundles, onion, and fennel. Wipe out Dutch oven for next step.

Heat two of the tablespoons of oil in the Dutch oven over medium-high heat. Add carrots and diced fennel bulb. Season with salt to taste. Cover, and cook for eight minutes stirring occasionally. The carrots and fennel will begin to caramelize. That's OK.

Add the diced white onion and cook, covered, for another five minutes or until onion is soft and bottom of pan is browning. Add the six cloves of minced garlic, and cook one minute more. It should start to really smell good at this point.

Remove pot from heat and stir in vinegar. Use a spatula to scrape up any browned (caramelized!) bits of onion stuck to the bottom. Add beans, chopped thyme, two tablespoons of the chopped parsley, and 1½ to two cups bean cooking liquid. The total liquid in the pot should come to just above top of beans; add more if necessary. Stir well to combine.

Prepare a 9x13-inch baking pan with cooking spray. Pour bean mixture into pan and spread out evenly. Combine breadcrumbs and remaining chopped parsley in small bowl. Drizzle remaining one tablespoon oil into crumb mixture, and combine to moisten breadcrumbs. Spread breadcrumb mixture over the top of the bean mixture. Cover and freeze.

To serve, unthaw completely and bake, uncovered, at 375 degrees for 40 to 45 minutes, or until top is browned and juices have bubbled down below the surface, leaving brown rim around edge of crust.

Remove from oven and cool for at least 15 minutes to allow beans to finish absorbing juices. Serve warm with lots of fresh homemade rolls or slices of a good store-bought French bread.

7   Hearty Kale & Sausage Turnovers

The term 'turnover' has different meanings depending on its use. It means one thing to accountants, another to human resource managers, and still another to financial advisors.

To foodies, a turnover is a small pastry made by covering one half of a piece of dough with a filling, folding the other half over on top, and sealing the edges. They are a hearty and tasty wintertime favorite in our home. The vegetarian sausage provides the "hearty". The combination of kale, onions, apples, and golden raisins provides the "tasty".

Although this recipe takes approximately 30 minutes of prep time I am confident that your time will be well spent. Serve warm turnovers for lunch or as a lite supper with a simple salad on the side.

Dough ingredients:
2½ cups flour
1 cup unsalted butter (cut into small pieces)
1½ teaspoons salt
½ cup ice water

Filling ingredients:
1 tablespoon extra-virgin olive oil
1 package Lightlife Italian Smart Sausages
1 medium onion (medium dice)
2 Granny Smith apples (core but do no peel; medium dice)
1 bunch kale (ribs removed; chop remaining leaves)

¼ cup golden raisins
Salt and fresh ground pepper to taste

Directions:
In a large mixing bowl, combine flour, butter, and salt. Cut butter into flour/salt until the mixture resembles coarse corn meal. Add ice water, one tablespoon at a time, to mixture stirring constantly until dough holds together. Form dough into a disk and wrap tightly. Place in refrigerator while preparing the sausage filling.

In a large skillet, heat oil over medium-high. Add sausage, cover and cook for five minutes. Remove from skillet and chop coarsely. Add back to skillet along with onions and cook until onions are translucent: another five minutes. Add apple, kale and raisins. Cover and cook until kale is almost tender; about five minutes. Uncover and season with salt and pepper to taste. Set aside.

Roll out dough on a lightly floured surface to 1/8-inch thickness. With a small bowl, cut out 6-inch rounds. This should make eight nice turnovers when filled. Place ½ cup sausage mixture on one side of each round. Rub a little water around the edge and fold over to form half-moons. Using a fork, press edges firmly to seal. Place turnovers on a parchment-lined baking sheet and freeze.

To serve, unthaw and make a ½-inch cross cut on the top of each turnover. Bake at 400 degrees for 25 to 30 minutes or until golden brown and crisp. Remove from oven and cool on a wire rack for three to five minutes before serving.

If you like gravy with your turnovers, buy two packages of your favorite package of gravy mix at the store and cook according to directions.

8   Hearty Quinoa Burger

Are you tired of the mass-produced veggie burger patties found at your favorite grocery store? Tired of the garden burgers foisted on you as the only choice at your favorite drive-thru? Take a look at the quinoa burger recipe below.

This one is delicious, nutritious, and wonderfully different. This one's a winner.

Ingredients:
15-ounce can kidney beans (rinsed and mashed)
2 egg whites (lightly beaten)
1 shallot (minced)
1 carrot (grated)
3 tablespoons Queso Cotija cheese (crumbled)
2 tablespoons cilantro (chopped fine)
1 teaspoon salt
3 cups quinoa (cooked according to package directions)
¼ cup vegetable oil
Iceberg lettuce
1 small red onion (sliced thin)
2 avocados (peeled, seeds removed and sliced)
4 Kaiser rolls (sliced in half horizontally)
Dijon mustard
Vegenaise (or mayonnaise)

Directions:
Add mashed kidney beans, egg whites, shallot, carrot, cheese, cilantro, and salt to a large mixing bowl. Stir to combine. Drain any excess water from the cooked quinoa and add to this mixture. Stir to combine quinoa.

Form quinoa mixture into four 1-inch thick patties. You may have some mixture left over. Make it into a patty and it will keep up to 4 or 5 days if sealed in a container and refrigerated.

Place the patties on a parchment-lined tray and cover. Put in the refrigerator to chill for at least 30 minutes before frying (if not chilled and firm they will disintegrate when frying).

Heat the oil in a skillet on medium-high heat. Cook patties for 4 to 5 minutes on each side. They should be crispy and golden in color. Drain patties of excess oil by placing between paper towels. Place in container and freeze.

To serve, unthaw the patties and reheat in a 300 degree oven for 15 minutes. While the patties are reheating, prepare the set ups.

The setups are easy. I learned how to do this as an inside worker at the Hayward A&W in the late 60s. Carefully break off a round leaf of head lettuce and place it curled-side up on the counter. Place a couple of onion slices on top of the lettuce and a few avocado slices on top of the onions. Do this three more times.

To prep the buns, spread mustard on the bottom half of each bun and Vegenaise on the other half. Now you're ready for the burger patties.

Place one reheated patty on the bottom half of each bun. Place one set up on each of the patties and complete each burger with the bun tops. Serve with chips on the side and a cold drink of your choice.

9 Jollof Rice Bowl

My friend asked me the other day if I had a recipe for jollof. I told her that I had heard of it, but had never made any. I was intrigued and told her I would check it out.

So, what is jollof? Jollof is a one-pot rice dish popular in many West Africa countries including Ghana and Nigeria. If it has a North American equivalent, you could loosely say it is similar to jambalaya without the celery.

Spicy and colorful, jollof is fun to bring to the table where it is sure to elicit oohs and aahs. My recipe includes slices of sausage (vegetarian sausage, of course). You can leave the sausage out, but it turns a side dish into a hearty meal. I like to remove the seeds from the habanero pepper but if you like super spicy rice, leave the seeds in!

Ingredients:
3 links of Lightlife Italian Smart Sausages (cut into ½-inch thick pieces)
¼ cup extra-virgin olive oil plus 1 teaspoon (divided)
4 medium red bell peppers (sliced fine)
2 large sweet onions (fine dice)
3 cloves garlic (minced)
2 teaspoons salt
1 Habanero pepper (deveined, seeded sliced thin)
4 ounces plum tomatoes (medium dice)
1 teaspoon dried thyme
½ teaspoon ground ginger
½ teaspoon Aleppo pepper

½ teaspoon smoked paprika
1 heaping teaspoon tomato paste
2½ cups vegetable broth
1¼ cups basmati rice

Directions:
Using a nonstick pan, fry the sausage over medium-high heat for two minutes. Turn each slice over and continue frying for two minutes more. Cover, remove from heat, and set aside.

Using a 4-quart saucepan, sauté the peppers and onions in the oil over medium-high heat for about five minutes, stirring frequently. Add garlic, salt, habanero pepper, tomatoes, and dry seasonings (thyme thru paprika) and cook for another 10 minutes over medium heat, stirring on occasion. Add the tomato paste, cook for 60 seconds more.

Stir the vegetable broth and oil into the pepper/onion mixture. Heat over medium-high heat until it begins to bubble. Add rice and stir to combine. Cover and simmer for 10 minutes. Open the lid and stir gently, but thoroughly, again. Cover and simmer for another 10 minutes. Open and stir for a final time, then simmer for a final 10 minutes.

Turn the heat off and allow to steam, covered, for another 10 minutes. Keeping it covered while it cools improves the final taste and texture of the rice. Take off the cover and let heat escape for five minutes. Fluff with a fork to separate the rice, slowly working inward from the edge of the pan in a swirling motion. Gently fold sausage into cooked rice and spoon into container. Freeze until ready to reheat.

To reheat, unthaw and bake, uncovered, for 15 to 20 minutes at 325 degrees.

Tip: This recipe makes a generous amount for two and may be doubled to feed four.

10   Lemony Artichoke Turnovers

Looking for a tasty appetizer for dinner? Look no further. This recipe takes a bit of prep time but is not hard to make. The combination of artichoke hearts and cheeses is classic and with the shallots, garlic and wine, make a wonderful filling for the crispy puff pastry. Perfect finger food.

Ingredients:
4 tablespoons unsalted butter
1 large shallot (minced)
3 cloves garlic (minced)
3 tablespoons flour (plus more for surface)
½ cup dry white wine
½ cup warm milk
½ cup warm vegetable broth
1 teaspoon salt
Fresh ground pepper to taste
Pinch of cayenne pepper
14-oz can artichoke bottoms (drained and chopped)
½ cup Parmesan cheese (finely grated)
½ cup Pecorino Romano cheese (finely grated)
1 tablespoon fresh thyme (chopped fine)
1½ teaspoons lemon zest (chopped fine)
1 teaspoon Dijon mustard
4 sheets puff pastry (unthawed)

Directions:
Melt butter in a small saucepan over medium heat. Cook shallot and garlic for one minute. Add flour, and cook, stirring constantly, for two minutes. Add wine, and cook until reduced by half, about two minutes. Whisk in milk and broth. Bring to a boil. Season with one teaspoon salt, pepper to taste, and the cayenne. Simmer until thickened, about two minutes. Remove from heat, and stir in artichoke hearts, cheeses, thyme, zest, and mustard. Let cool completely.

On a lightly floured surface, roll out each sheet of puff pastry to a 1/8-inch thickness. Cut each of the four sheets into nine 3-inch squares.

Arrange 1 tablespoon artichoke mixture in center of each square. Fold over to form a triangle with remaining edges, pressing to seal. Transfer to a parchment-lined baking sheet. Repeat with remaining dough and filling. Cover and freeze.

To serve, unthaw and make two or three small scores across the top of each turnover to vent steam. Bake in a 400 degree oven until golden, about 20 minutes.

11 Malt Ball Cupcakes

I remember my first taste of a malt. I was 12 years old and sitting at the Woolworth's lunch counter in Hayward with my mom and brother. Woolworth's was on 'The Strip' in downtown Hayward. This was before the modern mall was built outside of town in the early '60s. 'The Strip' was the place to be.

Don't know what dad was doing that Saturday but he missed out. Mom ordered three grilled-cheese sandwiches, a basket of fries, three glasses of water, and a chocolate malted milkshake. The three of us took turns sipping the shake through a straw. You had to really such hard to get the thick shake through the straw but when you did it was heaven. The straws were made of paper then, so by the time we finished the milkshake we had gone through a number of paper straws. We had tons of fun that afternoon.

I should have titled this recipe either, *Bring Out the Inner Kid in You,* or *How to Have Fun with Chocolate*. Malt Ball Cupcakes are what I want for my birthday every year until I am no more. They can be my dinner, and my birthday cake all rolled in one. They are that good and they freeze well until you want them.

Cupcake Ingredients:
6 tablespoons butter
1/3 cup vegetable oil
¾ cup water
1½ cups flour
1½ cups sugar

½ cup unsweetened cocoa powder
½ cup malted milk powder
1 teaspoon baking soda
¼ teaspoon salt
2 eggs
1/3 cup buttermilk
1½ teaspoon vanilla
Malt Ball Frosting *

Cupcake Directions:
Preheat oven to 350 degrees. Line 24 muffin cups with paper liners.

Heat butter, oil and water in a small saucepan over medium heat until butter is melted. Set aside.

Stir together flour, sugar, cocoa powder, malted milk powder, baking soda, and salt in a large bowl with electric mixer. Add butter mixture and beat until combined. Beat in eggs, one at a time, then stir in buttermilk and vanilla.

Pour batter into prepared muffin cups and bake for about 20 minutes or until a toothpick inserted into the center comes out clean. Cool completely before frosting. Place in container (frosting and all) and freeze.

To serve, unthaw and let come to room temperature.

*Frosting Ingredients:
1/3 cup butter (softened)
3 tablespoons malted milk powder

3½ cups powdered sugar
4 tablespoons milk
5-ounce package malted milk balls

*Frosting Directions:
Beat butter until creamy. Beat malted milk powder and add powdered sugar alternately with milk until mixture is smooth and spreadable. Set aside 24 whole malted milk balls from the 5-oz. package. Crush remaining malt balls coarsely and stir into frosting. Spread frosting over cupcakes and top with a whole malt ball.

12 Marinara Sauce *VEGAN*

Use this sauce with my Eggplant Parmigiano-Reggiano (4) recipe or keep it in the freezer for quick and easy spaghetti dinners.

Ingredients:
½ cup extra-virgin olive oil
2 small onions (chopped fine)
2 garlic cloves (chopped fine)
2 stalks celery chopped fine)
2 carrots (scrubbed clean and chopped fine)
½ teaspoon salt
½ teaspoon freshly ground black pepper
2 28-ounce cans crushed tomatoes
2 dried bay leaves

Directions:
In a large casserole pot, heat the oil over a medium-high flame. Add the onions, and garlic, and sauté until the onions are translucent - about 10 minutes. Add the celery, carrots, and ½ teaspoon of each salt and pepper. Sauté until all the vegetables are soft, about 10 minutes. Add the tomatoes and bay leaves, and simmer uncovered over low heat until the sauce thickens, about 1 hour.

Remove from heat and discard the bay leaf. Season the sauce with more salt if needed. Cover and freeze.

To serve, unthaw and place in a large saucepan. Reheat over medium heat for 15 minutes or until it starts to bubble around the edges.

13 Black Beans, Chard and Sorghum Bowl

When cooked in vegetable broth with a few sprigs of the Mexican herb epazote, the black beans and sorghum in this recipe will put a smile on your face. Together they are a magic combination that makes your belly sigh with contentment. *"Thank you,"* it will say, *"for making something healthy for dinner tonight."*

But wait. There's more. Swiss chard is one of the world's healthiest vegetables providing goodly amount of vitamins C, K, and A. It also has a healthy helping of magnesium, manganese, and potassium. The addition of avocado, which is cholesterol and sodium-free, provides 3.5 grams of "good fat" per 1 ounce serving. What's not to like about that?

Put succinctly, this dish is not only healthy but super tasty too!

Ingredients:
½ cup sorghum
2 cups vegetable broth
1 cup water
2 large sprigs epazote *
1 tablespoon coconut oil
1 small white onion (chopped)
2 cloves garlic (minced)
1 large Jalapeño chile (chopped fine)
1 bunch red Swiss chard (ribs removed and leaves chopped)
⅓ cup cilantro leaves (chopped)
1 teaspoon lime juice

2 15-ounce cans black beans (drained)
1 large avocado (diced for garnish)
2 to 3 ounces Queso Fresco (crumbled for garnish)

Directions:
Combine sorghum, broth, water, and epazote in a saucepan. Add a pinch of salt and bring to a boil. Reduce the heat, cover and simmer 70 minutes or until sorghum is tender. Pick out epazote sprigs and discard. Retain liquid, cover and set aside.

Heat the coconut oil over medium heat in a large skillet then add the onion and garlic. Cook for five minutes. Add the Jalapeño, chard, cilantro, and lime juice and cover. Cook for another five minutes. Remove from heat and set aside.

Add the beans to the saucepan with the sorghum. Add an additional ¼ cup water if needed. Cook for an additional 10 minutes on medium high. Remove from heat and allow to cool.

Combine onion/chard mixture with the beans and stir to combine. Spoon into a freezer-safe container and freeze.

To serve, completely unthaw. Place the unthawed beans in a large soup pan or pot and cook for 15 minutes on medium heat, or until it begins to bubble on the sides and is heated through.

Divide the beans among four bowls. Garnish with avocado and Queso Fresco.

Tip: If you don't have access to epazote, substitute two teaspoons dried Mexican oregano.

14 Oatmeal Bread

Oat grouts are coarsely ground to make oatmeal or cut into small pieces to make steel-cut oats, or first steamed and then flattened to make rolled oats. Bet you didn't know all that! Can't say I did until I looked it up on-line.

This recipe uses quick cooking oats (oat grouts cut into small pieces before being steamed and rolled) and makes a sweet oatmeal bread. I serve it at dinnertime or enjoy it, as a snack, with a cup of coffee or tea.

Ingredients:
1½ cups boiling water
1 cup quick cooking oats
½ cup vegetable oil
1 cup brown sugar
2 eggs
½ teaspoon nutmeg
1 teaspoon baking soda
1 cup sugar
1 teaspoon cinnamon
½ teaspoon salt
1 1/3 cup flour

Directions:
Preheat oven to 350 degrees.

Combine boiling water, oats, and oil. Allow to cool after stirring a couple of times. In a separate bowl, combine brown sugar, eggs, nutmeg, baking soda, sugar, cinnamon, and salt. Slowly stir in flour until mixture fully forms.

Add the two mixtures together. Grease a large loaf pan and add mixture to the pan. Bake for 65 – 70 minutes. Remove from oven and allow to cool. Remove from pan and place in a large baggie or seal in plastic wrap then freeze.

To serve, remove from freezer and allow to unthaw at room temperature. This may take five to eight hours. Cut into slices and serve with breakfast, dinner, or lunch!

15 Orzo Pasta with Asiago Cheese

The word *orzo* is Italian for barley and a reference to its size and shape. Orzo may look like a large grain of rice but it is a form of short pasta used in a variety of recipes including salads and soups.

Asiago cheese, pronounced *ah-SYAH-goh*, is a hard cow's milk cheese that is easy to grate. True Asiago must be made in the alpine regions of Veneto and Trentino, Italy. Asiago cheese is an Italian PDO (Protected Designation of Origin), which means that it has to be produced in a designated region in a particular way to be considered the real thing. If you buy Asiago that bears the brand of the Asiago consortium on the rind, you know that the cheese was made with milk from cows that graze on the grassy hillsides of the Italian Dolomite Mountains.

This combination of orzo and aged Asiago cheese makes a different and very tasty pasta side dish.

Ingredients:
4 tablespoons sweet butter
2 cups orzo pasta
28 ounces vegetable broth
2 teaspoons Better Than Bouillon Vegetable Base
1 cup aged Asiago cheese (grated)
2 tablespoons dried basil
Cracked black pepper to taste

Directions:
Prepare a 9x9-inch baking pan with cooking spray.

Melt butter in a 4-quart pan over medium-high heat. Add orzo pasta and stir until browned. Do not allow to burn. Stir in vegetable broth, Better Than Bouillon, and cover. Reduce heat to low and simmer for 15 minutes. Uncover and stir once. Continue cooking, uncovered, for five additional minutes or until all liquid is absorbed.

Remove orzo from heat and stir in Asiago cheese. Season with cracked pepper to taste. Pour into prepared baking pan and cover with aluminum foil. Allow to cool for five minutes before putting in freezer.

To serve, unthaw completely. Then, set the oven to 325 degrees and heat uncovered for approximately 15 minutes or until heated through. This is a nice side dish, or when accompanied by a tossed salad, becomes a filling entrée for four people.

16 Quinoa and Chik'n Casserole *VEGAN*

When my young 12-year old friend saw me preparing this for our family and his, he asked, *How the heck can you make enchiladas in a slow cooker? That just doesn't sound right.*

I like that all of the ingredients in the slow cooker come together for a taste that is amazingly good and, unlike traditional enchiladas, is a lot easier to make. When my friend tasted this slow cooker vegan enchilada dish at dinnertime he exclaimed, *Amazing! You can make this for mom and me anytime.*

Ingredients:
2 packages Quorn Vegan Chik'n Tenders
1½ cups uncooked quinoa (such as Bob's Red Mill)
15-ounce can black beans (drained and rinsed)
2 cobs of fresh corn (shuck and slice off corn)
15-ounce can diced fire roasted tomatoes
2 cloves garlic (minced)
1 medium white onion (chopped)
2 Jalapeño peppers (seeded and chopped)
2½ cups water
10-ounce can red enchilada sauce (such as Old El Paso)
2 tablespoons chili powder
1 tablespoon cumin
2 teaspoons ground coriander
Salt to taste
1½ cups shredded Mexican blend cheese
3 green onions (chopped for garnish)
¼ cup fresh cilantro (chopped for garnish)

Directions:
Plug in and set slow cooker to high.

Add the first 13 ingredients (Quorn through coriander) to a slow cooker. Stir to combine. Cover and cook for three hours.

Remove the lid and stir everything again. Taste and adjust for salt if necessary. Stir in cheese and transfer to a container for freezing.

To serve, unthaw completely. Heat over medium heat for about 25 minutes or until edges bubble and is warmed through. Ladle into bowls and sprinkle each bowl with green onions and cilantro. Serve with warm corn tortillas on the side.

17 Tempeh Salisbury Steak

Ever wonder about the origin of Salisbury steak? As a kid I thought it was created for frozen "TV Dinners", a staple of my brother's and my diet in the 1960s. Here's the real origin of Salisbury Steak according to FoodReference.com:

> One of the earliest of the health food fadists, Dr. James H. Salisbury, a 19th century English/American physician (1823-1905), wrote <u>The Relation of Alimentation and Disease</u>. Salisbury believed that diet was the main factor governing our health, so he created a special food and diet for his patients suffering from anemia, colitis, gout, rheumatism, arteriosclerosis, tuberculosis, and asthma.

He claimed our teeth are "meat teeth" and our digestive systems designed to digest lean meat, and that vegetables, fats, starches and fruit should only be 1a third of our diet. Starch was digested slowly, so it would ferment in the stomach and produce vinegar, acid, alcohol, and yeast, all of which were poisonous to our systems. His cure for this was his special diet, including Salisbury Steak, which should be eaten three times a day, together with lots of hot water to rinse out the digestive system.

I adapted a Salisbury Steak recipe to work with tempeh, added some gravy, and before you could say *Swanson's*, I had something nutritional, and tasty. I think Dr. Salisbury would approve of this recipe.

Ingredients:
4 tablespoons extra-virgin olive oil
1 1/3 cups onion (chopped fine – divided)
2 slices white bread
½ cup milk
16 ounces organic tempeh (steamed and cut into ¼-inch dice)
2 garlic cloves (minced)
1 large egg
2 tablespoons Italian parsley (chopped)
2 teaspoons vegetarian Worcestershire sauce
2 teaspoons salt
¼ teaspoon freshly ground black pepper
1 teaspoon cornstarch plus ¼ cup for "dusting"

1½ cups vegetable broth

Directions:
Steam tempeh for nine minutes. Remove from steamer and cut into ¼-inch dice. Set aside.

Heat a skillet over medium heat. Add two tablespoons of the oil and one cup of the onions. Reduce heat to medium-low, and cook, stirring occasionally, until onions are golden brown and caramelized - about 10 minutes. Set aside.

Soak bread briefly in milk and chop fine. In a large bowl, combine the tempeh, remaining 1/3 cup raw onions, garlic, bread, egg, parsley, Worcestershire sauce, salt, and pepper. Mix with your hands to combine. Divide tempeh mixture into six oblong patties. Dust both sides of patties with the ¼ cup of cornstarch.

Heat a large skillet over medium–high heat. Add remaining two tablespoons oil and reduce heat to medium. Cook patties for six minutes on medium heat without moving them, then flip and cook them for another nine minutes. Set patties aside on a plate.

Add cooked onions and one teaspoon cornstarch to same skillet and stir for one minute. Raise heat to medium-high. Pour in broth and whisk until broth is clear and slightly thickened - about three minutes. Remove pan with sauce from heat. Set aside.

Lay patties in a freezable container. Pour sauce over patties, cover, and freeze.

To serve, unthaw completely and place in 350 degree oven for 15 to 20 minutes or until bubbly and heated through. Serve with mashed potatoes and fresh green beans for a complete vegetarian TV-Dinner.

18 Bread Pudding

The origin of bread pudding is uncertain. Cooks from many countries and cultures, not wanting to waste stale bread, invented many uses for it including pudding. Today's bread pudding shares these humble roots and adds a few twists (depending upon the cook). Some cooks make it with day-old donuts but I prefer day-old French bread. I also like to add apples, walnuts, and molasses to mine, and serve it with a tasty whiskey sauce*.

This can be served any time of the day. I especially enjoy it for a weekend breakfast.

Bread Pudding Ingredients:
¼ cup unsalted butter
3 Granny Smith apples (peeled and diced)
1½ cups sugar (divided)
2 tablespoons molasses
¼ cup raisins
¼ cup walnuts (chopped)
1 teaspoon vanilla (divided)
½ teaspoon cinnamon
3 large eggs
1 cup milk
2 cups heavy cream
1/8 teaspoon nutmeg
6 cups bread cubes (I cut up day-old French bread into 1-inch cubes)

Bread Pudding Directions:
Preheat oven to 350 degrees. Prepare a casserole dish with cooking spray.

Melt butter in saucepan. Add apples, ¾ cup sugar, molasses, raisins, walnuts, ½ teaspoon of the vanilla and all of the cinnamon. Stir to incorporate, remove from heat and set aside.

Lightly beat eggs in a bowl. Add milk, cream, the balance of the sugar and the balance of the vanilla. Add nutmeg and set aside.

Place bread cubes in a large mixing bowl. Add apple and custard mixtures. Mix thoroughly. Spoon bread mixture into the casserole dish and bake for 45 to 60 minutes or until pudding appears solid and light brown. Remove from oven and allow to cool. Cover and freeze.

To serve, remove from the freezer and allow to thaw completely. Place bread pudding (covered) in the oven and bake at 350 degrees for about 15 minutes or until heated through.

*Serve pudding with the following sauce. Make it while the bread pudding is reheating.

Whiskey Sauce Ingredients:
2 cups heavy cream
½ cup whole milk
½ cup sugar
2 tablespoons cornstarch
¾ cup Jack Daniels whiskey
Pinch of salt

Sauce Directions:

In a 1-quart saucepan set over medium heat, combine the cream, milk, and sugar. Place the cornstarch and ¼ cup of the whiskey in a small mixing bowl and whisk until blended. Pour this into the cream mixture and bring to a boil. Once the sauce begins to boil, reduce the heat to a gentle simmer and cook, stirring occasionally, for five minutes. Remove the sauce from the heat, add a pinch of salt and the remaining ½ cup of whiskey. Stir to combine and ladle over each piece of bread pudding before serving.

19 Vegetarian Jambalaya

I was asked the other day if I had a recipe for vegetarian jambalaya. I said, *Yes,* and then asked, *do you need the recipe right now so you can make it for dinner tonight?* My friend replied that she wanted to make it this weekend, when she had more time to cook, and then freeze it for dinner on the following Wednesday. I assured her that I had the perfect make-ahead recipe and that I would email it to her as soon as I got home.

Since my recipe does not contain meat or shrimp, I add vegetarian sausage. It provides flavor, and a robustness not found in other vegetarian jambalaya recipes. I also add two types of beans for extra protein and texture. Here's the recipe I sent to my friend:

Ingredients:
1 tablespoon extra-virgin olive oil
2 links Lightlife Italian Smart Sausages (cut into ½-inch slices)
1 yellow onion (medium chop)
1 green bell pepper (medium chop)
½ cup celery (medium chop)
3 cloves garlic (minced)
2 cups vegetable broth
14 ounce can fire-roasted diced tomatoes (undrained)
8 ounce can tomato sauce
2 teaspoons Cajun seasoning (or use my recipe below* to make your own)
1 cup uncooked long grain rice

15 ounce can cannellini beans (rinsed and drained)
15 ounce can small red beans (such as Goya brand: rinsed and drained)

Directions:
In a large skillet, heat oil over medium heat. Sauté sausage, onion, bell pepper, celery, and garlic for five to six minutes, stirring frequently. Add broth, tomatoes, tomato sauce, and Cajun seasoning.

Bring to a boil and add rice. Reduce heat to low, cover and simmer for 20 to 25 minutes until rice is tender, stirring occasionally. Add beans, ¼ cup of water, cover, and simmer for 10 minutes stirring occasionally. Remove from heat and allow to cool for 10 minutes. Spoon into container and freeze.

To serve, remove frozen jambalaya from freezer and unthaw completely. Place unthawed jambalaya in a large skillet. Add 3 tablespoons of water to skillet and cook, covered, for about 15 minutes on medium heat or until heated through.

*Cajun Seasoning Ingredients:
1 tablespoon garlic powder
1 tablespoon onion powder
1 tablespoon dried oregano
1 tablespoon dried basil
1½ tablespoon dried thyme
1 tablespoon fresh ground black pepper
1 teaspoon cayenne pepper
3 tablespoons paprika
2 tablespoons seasoning salt

*Cajun Seasoning Directions:
With this recipe, there is no need for a mortar and pestle or for a blender. Place all ingredients in a jar with a tight-fitting lid and shake to combine. Store in the refrigerator to keep it fresh.

20 Veggie Meatballs

You might very well ask whether vegetarian meatballs is an oxymoron. I would answer yes to that. I would also add that their hearty texture, and rich taste, is actually preferred over real meatballs by most of my meat-eating friends.

This recipe takes planning ahead, as the balls need to be frozen before they bake. Your efforts, however, will be well worth it. Serve these as a main course with rice or with whole-wheat noodles. I like them served over thin spaghetti. They can also be served alongside turkey at Thanksgiving, and other celebrations, to the delight of everyone.

Ingredients:
Meatballs:
2½ cups cracker crumbs
2½ cups walnuts (chopped)
1 teaspoon seasoning salt
3 teaspoons dried sage
1 large onion (chopped fine)
1½ cups Longhorn cheese (grated)
6 tablespoons fresh parsley (minced)
8 large eggs
pinch of garlic powder

Sauce:
6 green onions (chopped)
1 clove garlic (crushed)
1 tablespoon butter (margarine substitutes nicely)
2 cans mushroom soup
16 ounces sour cream

Directions:

Mix together cracker crumbs, walnuts, seasonings, onion, cheese, parsley, eggs and garlic powder. Form into balls approximately 1½-inches in diameter. Place balls on baking sheet and freeze.

To serve, remove veggie meatballs from freezer but do not unthaw. Place in a 9x13-inch baking dish. Set aside.

Sauté green onions and garlic in butter. Add soup and sour cream. Stir to combine and then pour over balls. Cover with foil and bake for 45 minutes. Serve "bubbling" hot.

Refrigerator Recipes

[Robin's Tortilla Soup]

21 Asparagus and Gruyère Quiche

Looking for something new to take on a picnic? Look no further. This quiche has body and, just as important, an amazing combination of flavors that pair with most anything you add to your picnic basket.

Gruyère is a hard yellow cheese named after the town of Gruyère in Switzerland. It is sweet but slightly salty, with a flavor that varies widely with age. It is often described as creamy and nutty when young, becoming with age more assertive, earthy and complex. This recipe takes advantage of aging. The flavor and texture of my whole wheat crust adds yet another dimension of flavor that will make you yodel with delight.

Crust Ingredients:
1½ cups whole wheat flour
1½ cups white flour
1 cup wheat germ
1½ teaspoon sea salt
1 cup plus 4 tablespoons butter
10 – 12 tablespoons cold water

Filling Ingredients:
1 tablespoon butter
1 leek (white and light green parts only - halved and thinly sliced)
1 pound asparagus (tough ends removed stems sliced thin diagonally)
4 large eggs
1¼ cups half-and-half

½ teaspoon salt
½ teaspoon fresh ground pepper
Pinch of ground nutmeg
1 cup aged Gruyère cheese (grated)

Crust Directions:
Stir together flour, wheat germ and salt. Cut butter into these dry ingredients (a pastry cutter makes this easy). When the dough is the consistency of rolled oats, sprinkle with enough of the water to hold the dough together. Form into a ball, cover and refrigerate for about an hour while you prepare the filling.

Filling Directions:
In a large skillet, melt butter over medium heat. Add leek and asparagus; season with salt and pepper. Cook, stirring occasionally, until asparagus is tender - about seven or eight minutes. Set aside to cool. In a medium bowl, whisk together eggs, half-and-half, salt, pepper and nutmeg. Set aside.

Baking Directions:
Prepare a 9x9-inch square baking pan with cooking spray.

Roll out dough and lay carefully in the baking pan creating a 1½-inch high crust up the sides of the pan. Sprinkle Gruyère on bottom of crust and top with asparagus/leek mixture. Pour egg mixture on top. Bake until center of quiche is set – about 50 minutes. Allow to cool, then cover and refrigerate.

To serve, preheat oven to 350 degrees. Bake room temperature quiche, uncovered, for 15 to 20 minutes or until heated through.

22 Back-to-Our Root Vegetables

Parsnips, rutabagas and the like are common fare in Norway. Although it may be a clumsy play on words, I call this the "back to our roots" recipe. Here's why.

My grandfather's "grandfather", Amund Eidsmoe, came to America in 1852 from Norway settling in southeastern South Dakota. It was there that my grandfather (Gramps) was born and later met and married my grandmother (Gran). Living in a home that had a root cellar with carrots, parsnips, rutabagas and potatoes was not uncommon in those days. In fact, root cellars often made it possible to eat well during the harsh winter months.

When Gran and Gramps moved to California during the Great Depression, Gran continued to cook from recipes that were passed down to her by my grandfather's side of the family. In addition to making a wonderful carrot casserole for us each fall, Gran would make this inexpensive vegetable bake at the first hint of cool weather.

Ingredients:
1 pound organic carrots (scrubbed and cut into ½ inch lengths)
1 pound new potatoes (quartered – scrub but no need to peel)
1 pound organic parsnips (peeled and cut into ½ inch lengths)
1 pound organic rutabaga (peeled and diced cut into ½ inch cubes)
2 to 3 tablespoons extra-virgin olive oil

1½ teaspoons salt
½ teaspoon pepper
1 1/3 cups cream (milk or half and half will *not* do!)
1 1/3 cups Fontina cheese
1 tablespoon parsley (chopped)
2 tablespoons finely grated Parmesan cheese
1 tablespoon breadcrumbs

Directions:
Preheat oven to 400 degrees.

Place prepared root vegetables (carrots through rutabaga) in a large baking dish (I use a tall Corning Ware 2.8 liter dish). Drizzle with olive oil, salt and pepper. Toss to coat. Roast vegetables uncovered for 1 hour and 10 minutes.

Transfer roasted vegetables to a large mixing bowl. Stir in cream, Fontina and ½ of the parsley. Transfer vegetable mixture back to baking dish. Sprinkle top with Parmesan cheese, breadcrumbs and balance of the parsley. Cover and freeze.

To serve, bake for 10 to 15 minutes at 350 degrees or until bubbly hot.

23 Burrata Lasagna

What is Burrata? Burrata a semisoft white Italian cheese made from mozzarella and cream. The outer shell is solid mozzarella, while the inside contains both mozzarella and cream, giving it an unusual texture. It is to die for.

What is lasagna? I say it is the ultimate one-pot meal. In its most basic form, lasagna is a layered dish of long, wide noodles with blankets of sauce, cheese, and other tasty ingredients in between. When you use Burrata cheese in lasagna the end result is amazing.

This is a make-ahead recipe, if you want, for two hungry adults. Make it the night before you need it, cover and put in the refer until ready to bake the next day.

Ingredients:
3 tablespoons unsalted butter (divided)
2 tablespoons olive oil (divided)
¾ pounds Chanterelle mushrooms (chopped)
¾ pounds Cremini mushrooms (chopped)
Salt and freshly ground pepper to taste
1 large shallot (chopped fine)
⅓ cup dry white wine
1 cup ricotta cheese
¼ cup heavy cream
12 lasagna noodles (cooked according to pkg directions)
2 4-ounce rounds Burrata cheese (torn into large pieces)

6 teaspoons Parmesan cheese (grated fine)
5 teaspoons fresh marjoram leaves

Directions:
Heat one tablespoon butter and one tablespoon oil in a large skillet over medium-high. Add Chanterelle mushrooms, season with salt and pepper and cook, stirring occasionally, until browned and starting to crisp – about 8 to 10 minutes. Transfer to a bowl and set aside.

Do the same with the Cremini mushrooms, 1 tablespoon butter and one tablespoon oil. Mix in first batch of mushrooms and add shallot, wine, and remaining one tablespoon butter. Cook, stirring occasionally, until mushroom mixture is considerably reduced - about five minutes. Return mushroom mixture to bowl and set aside.

Combine ricotta and cream in a small bowl. Season with salt and pepper and set aside.

Assembly:
There will be six layers of noodles. To begin, spread a thin layer of ricotta mixture in a small baking dish (I use a large bread loaf pan) and top with two noodles side by side. Spread $1/5^{th}$ of the ricotta mixture over noodles, layer with $1/5^{th}$ of the mushrooms, then a few pieces of Burrata.

Top evenly with 1 teaspoon Parmesan and one teaspoon marjoram leaves. Repeat layering process (starting with noodles and ending with marjoram) four more times. Dust the top with the last of the Parmesan and a bit of fresh ground pepper. Cover with foil and refrigerate.

To serve, bake at 425 degrees for 15 to minutes. Remove foil and continue baking until golden brown - about 10 minutes more. Serve with a fresh garden salad and vinaigrette dressing.

24 Cabbage and Chickpea Soup ^{VEGAN}

There's nothing quite like a hearty soup as the weather begins to cool down as soon as the sun sets. This soup is not only hearty but tasty AND nutritious. I also think you'll like how easy it is to prepare.

Ingredients:
2 teaspoons olive oil
1 onion (chopped)
1 garlic clove (crushed)
15-ounce can organic diced tomatoes
1 cup red cabbage (chopped)
1 cup green cabbage (chopped)
1 potato (diced)
¼ cup fresh parsley (finely chopped)
4 cups vegetable broth
1 tablespoon Better than Bouillon Vegetable Base
15-ounce can chickpeas (drained and rinsed)
1 teaspoon paprika
¼ teaspoon black pepper
Salt to taste

Directions:
Heat the oil in a large pot and sauté the onion until soft, about three to five minutes. Add the garlic, tomatoes, cabbage, potato, parsley, broth, garbanzo beans, paprika, and black pepper. Simmer until the potato and cabbage are tender, about 15 minutes.

Ladle approximately three cups of the soup into a blender. Starting on a low speed, blend until smooth, making sure to hold the lid on tightly. Return the blended soup to the pot and stir to mix, adding salt to taste. Cover and refrigerate.

To serve, reheat in a large soup pan over medium heat for 15 to 20 minutes or until edges start to bubble and soup is heated through. Serve with toast, crackers, or fresh bread rolls straight from the oven.

25 Chana Masala *VEGAN*

This vegan and gluten-free dish is a favorite of my friend Brandy. It is a savory dish of cooked garbanzo beans (chickpeas), onion, garlic, bay leaves and various Indian spices. It gets its heat from small red chiles and although I only use one chile in this recipe, you can add more if you like it hotter.

Ingredients:
2 tablespoons coconut oil
1 medium yellow onion (chopped fine)
1½ teaspoons ground coriander
1 teaspoon ground cumin
1 teaspoon turmeric
2 bay leaves
1 dried red chile (break in half)
1 cinnamon stick (break in half)
1 clove garlic (minced)
2 plum tomatoes (chopped)
2 15-ounce cans chickpeas (rinsed and drained)
1 tablespoon fresh ginger (grated)
1 cup vegetable broth *
Salt to taste
1 teaspoon garam masala
½ cup cilantro (chopped for garnish)

Directions:
Heat coconut oil in a large skillet over medium heat. Add the onion and cook, stirring, until soft, about five minutes. Stir in the coriander, cumin, turmeric, bay leaves, chile, cinnamon, and garlic. Cook until fragrant, about 1 minute more.

Add the tomatoes and cook until almost dry, about two minutes. Add the chickpeas, ginger, broth, and a pinch of salt. Reduce heat to medium-low, cover and cook, stirring occasionally, until the flavors meld and a thick sauce forms, about 15 minutes.

Remove and discard the bay leaves, chile, and cinnamon stick. Stir in the garam masala. Cover and refrigerate.

To serve, reheat in a large saucepan over medium heat for about 15 minutes or until bubbly. Pour into a serving dish and garnish with cilantro. Serve over rice or with rice on the side.

* I don't care for dry chana masala. If you like it on the dry side, reduce the broth to ½ cup.

26 Cheesy-Creamy Cauliflower

Get all the creamy, cheesy goodness of macaroni and cheese, without the high starch content of macaroni. This is a wonderful winter or early spring entrée that only needs a fresh garden salad to be a complete meal.

Ingredients:
8 cups cauliflower florets
2 tablespoons butter
3 tablespoons flour
2 cups heavy cream
1 clove garlic (minced)
2 cups extra-sharp Cheddar cheese (grated)
½ cup nutritional yeast
1 pinch cayenne pepper
2 egg yolks
1½ cups fresh breadcrumbs

Directions:
Bring large pot of salted water to a boil. Add cauliflower florets, and boil 5 to 6 minutes or until just tender. Drain, *reserving 1 cup cooking liquid*, and set aside.

Melt butter in same pot over medium heat. Whisk in flour, and cook 1 minute, stirring constantly. Whisk in cream, garlic, and reserved cooking liquid. Cook for about 5 minutes, or until sauce is thickened, whisking constantly. Remove from heat. Stir in cheese, nutritional yeast, cayenne pepper, and egg yolks. Stir until cheese is melted. Fold in cauliflower.

Coat a 13x9-inch baking dish or pan with cooking spray. Spread cauliflower mixture in baking dish, and sprinkle with breadcrumbs (to make your own fresh breadcrumbs, tear firm, fresh bread into pieces and whirl in a food processor or blender until crumbs form). Cover and refrigerate.

To serve, bake uncovered for 30 minutes at 350 degrees or until casserole is hot and bubbly and breadcrumbs are crispy and brown.

Tip: for a change, substitute 1 cup Emmentaler and 1 cup Parmigiano-Reggiano for the Cheddar cheese.

27 Chickpea Veggie Patty Burger

There are many veggie burger recipes but our vegetarian son, Robert, and I prefer this one made with sprouted chickpeas. We made them during his visit over the holidays. Fresh, sprouted beans provide a number of micronutrients and are high in dietary fiber. They are also well known for being rich in iron. One cup, for example, provides 25% of your average daily iron needs.

If you can't find sprouted chickpeas you can substitute two cans of garbanzo beans. Make the patties a day or two ahead of time, store covered in the refrigerator and cook when you need them for a quick, nutritious meal. For a change, make them 2-½ to three inches in diameter and serve on a fresh mini bagel instead of a regular hamburger bun.

Ingredients:
2½ cups sprouted chickpeas
4 eggs
½ teaspoon salt
1/3 cup fresh cilantro (chopped)
1 medium white onion (chopped)
Grated zest of one large lemon
1 cup alfalfa sprouts (chopped)
1 cup toasted whole-grain breadcrumbs
1 tablespoon extra-virgin olive oil

Directions:

Steam the sprouted garbanzo beans until just tender - about 10 minutes. Combine the garbanzos, eggs, and salt in a food processor. Puree until the mixture is the consistency of a very thick, slightly chunky hummus. Pour into a mixing bowl and stir in the cilantro, onion, zest, and sprouts. Add the breadcrumbs, stir, and let sit for a couple of minutes so the crumbs can absorb some of the moisture.

At this point, you should have a moist mixture that you can easily form into one-inch thick patties. Robert and I like a nice, moist patty because it makes for a nicely textured burger. You can always add more breadcrumbs, a bit at a time, to firm up the dough if need be.

Heat the oil in a heavy skillet over medium low and cook patties for seven to 10 minutes, until the bottoms begin to brown. Turn up the heat if there is no browning after 10 minutes. Flip the patties and cook the second side for seven minutes more. Remove cooked patties from the skillet and cool on a wire rack while you cook the remaining patties. Transfer cooked patties to a container, cover, and refrigerate.

To serve, reheat the patties in the oven at 350 degrees for 15 minutes or until heated through. Serve with a standard setup of lettuce, tomato and onion, and don't forget your favorite secret sauce!

28 Collard Greens with Veggie Sausage

Collard greens are wonderfully low in calories, contain no cholesterol, and have a good amount of fiber. In addition, they are rich in vitamin-C, are an excellent source of vitamin-A, and have high levels of Vitamin-K. If that's not enough for you, the leaves and stems are good in minerals like iron, calcium, copper, manganese, selenium, and zinc.

This spicy recipe has great flavor and texture and, because it features collard greens, is an amazing source of nutrition.

Ingredients:
2 teaspoons extra-virgin olive oil
¼ teaspoon red chile pepper (crushed)
4 cloves garlic (minced)
1 medium onion (medium chop)
1 package Lightlife Italian Smart Sausages (cut into 1-inch pieces)
16 ounces fresh collard greens (remove stems and veins)
2 ½ tablespoons red wine vinegar
⅓ cup dry white wine
2 cups vegetable broth (boiling)
¾ cup tomato sauce
½ tablespoons dried thyme

Directions:

Heat oil and crushed pepper over medium-high heat in a very large saucepan or stockpot for one minute. Add garlic and onions. Cook for two minutes, and add sausage, stirring with a large spoon. Cook mixture for about five minutes, stirring frequently until sausages are browned.

Add collard greens, reduce heat to medium-low and cook mixture, covered, for five minutes. Add vinegar, wine, vegetable broth and tomato sauce. Reduce heat to low. Cover, and cook for 15 minutes. Add thyme, and cook five minutes longer, or until greens are tender, stirring occasionally. Cover and refrigerate.

To serve, reheat in a large saucepan over medium heat for 15 minutes or until bubbly. For a complete meal, serve with red beans and rice on the side.

29   Creamy Vodka Sauce

Robert first served this at a dinner he prepared for his friends at our home in Rocklin. Quick and easy to prepare, we like this sauce over penne pasta but it is equally good with linguini, gnocchi or another pasta of your choosing.

Ingredients:
2 tablespoon butter
1 tablespoon extra-virgin olive oil
1 medium onion (chopped)
1 28-ounce can Italian plum tomatoes (drained, seeded and chopped)
1½ cup heavy cream
1/3 cup basil-vodka
½ teaspoon dried crushed red pepper flakes
Salt and pepper (to taste)
Pasta (cooked according to package directions)

Directions:
Melt butter and olive oil in saucepan over medium heat. Add chopped onions and sauté about 6 minutes or until translucent. Add tomatoes and reduce until almost no liquid remains in pan; about 20 to 25 minutes. Be sure to stir frequently.

Add cream, vodka, and red pepper flakes. Cook for another two minutes. Season to taste with salt and pepper. Refrigerate until ready to use.

To serve, reheat in a saucepan over medium heat until sides begin to bubble and sauce is heated through – about 10 minutes. Serve over your favorite pasta.

30 Earthy Mushroom & Gruyère Quiche

This is not your ordinary quiche. What I like best about it is the combination of earthy baby Portobello mushrooms (Cremini) and nutty Gruyère cheese. Carefully layering the mushrooms and shredded Gruyère ensures consistently good flavor throughout.

When not making this as a refrigerator dish that is reheated the next day, I like to take this to potluck gatherings where it is always a hit. If paired with slightly chilled* Pinot Noir and a fresh garden salad, it is a complete and nutritious late lunch or early dinner.

Crust Ingredients:
¾ cup whole-wheat pastry flour
¼ cup flour
¼ cup whole ground flaxseed meal
⅛ teaspoon salt
2 tablespoons butter
2 tablespoons organic vegetable oil
5 tablespoons ice water

Filling Ingredients:
1 teaspoon extra-virgin olive oil
16 ounces Cremini mushrooms (sliced thickly)
1 small onion (chopped)
3 cloves garlic (minced)
1 tablespoon fresh thyme (chopped fine)
2 large eggs
3 egg whites
1½ cups milk (I use whole milk)

2 teaspoons Dijon mustard
¼ teaspoon grated fresh nutmeg
1 cup grated Gruyère cheese
Salt and pepper to taste

Directions:
Crust: Preheat oven to 425 degrees.

Whisk flours, flaxseed meal and salt together in a large bowl.

Heat butter in small skillet over low heat; cook until butter turns deep golden brown. Stir browned butter and oil into flour mixture with fork. Gradually stir in ice water until dough forms an easy-to-handle ball. Roll ball into 12-inch circle, and then press dough into a 9-inch spring form pan. Crimp dough at edges, and prick sides and bottom all over with fork. Pre-bake for 10 minutes at 425 degrees. Remove from oven to cool and reduce oven to 350 degrees.

Filling: Heat oil in large skillet over medium-high heat. Add mushrooms and onion; sauté eight minutes, or until browned and mushroom liquid has evaporated. Stir in garlic and thyme.

Whisk together eggs and egg whites in bowl. Whisk in milk, mustard, and nutmeg. Season with salt and pepper to taste.

Assembly: Sprinkle half of grated cheese on pre-baked crust. Top with mushroom mixture, then remaining cheese. Pour egg mixture over the top making sure mushrooms remain well-distributed in crust.

Bake completed quiche at 350 degrees for one hour or until firm. Let cool for about 10 minutes before wrapping and placing in refrigerator.

To reheat, set oven for 325 degrees. Bake for about 20 minutes or until heated through.

* By slightly chilled I mean 15 to 20 minutes in the refrigerator, no more.

31 Gran's Carrot Casserole

As a kid growing up in the San Francisco Bay Area, I enjoyed spending one week, just before the new school year, at my grandmother's house in Merced. I helped Gran pick peaches off the tree in the backyard and then watched her peel and can them for use throughout the year. Although Gran wasn't a good cook, I do remember one dish that I asked for every year. This was a carrot casserole she remembered her mom making for her when times were hard, and all they had to eat were root vegetables stored in the cellar.

Gran's original recipe was never written down but I remember the ingredients she used. One day, when I craved Gran's carrot casserole, I experimented until I got the right mix of ingredients. I hope you enjoy this simple dish as much as my family and I have enjoyed it over the years.

Ingredients:
1 small yellow onion (chopped fine)
½ cup butter
3 pounds carrots
¼ cup flour
1 egg
4 ounces Ritz crackers (crumbled)
¼ teaspoon salt
¼ teaspoon pepper

Directions:
Preheat oven to 350 degrees.

Sauté onion in butter until barely translucent. Take off heat and set aside. Scrub carrots. Do not peel. Cut carrots into 2-inch lengths. Steam until tender. Mash steamed carrots and add to onions. Cook over medium heat for five minutes. Transfer onion and carrot mixture to a large mixing bowl. Add flour, egg, cracker crumbs, salt and pepper. Mix well. Transfer mixture to a casserole dish or a loaf pan. Bake uncovered for one hour. Allow to cool before covering and placing in the refrigerator.

To reheat, set oven for 325 degrees. Bake for 20 minutes or until heated through. Gran served this dish with plain white rice and a fresh garden salad.

32 Hearty Chili Bean Soup *VEGAN*

I first developed this as a chili for the many chili cook-off events in which I've participated. Our son, Robert, helped serve at the cook-offs. Although the chili never won any awards, it was unique, interesting, and a welcome addition to the meaty chili dishes.

One rainy winter afternoon, I wanted hot soup but also had a hankering for chili beans. I dusted off my old Vegetarian Chili Beans recipe and tweaked it into a superb, hearty soup. This vegan recipe uses a slow cooker to maximize flavor.

Get it started at noontime and it will be ready for dinner or for refrigeration and reheating the next day. Serve with fresh, hot cornbread, and a garden salad for a completely nutritious and delicious meal.

Ingredients:
2 tablespoons extra-virgin olive oil
1 large onion (chopped)
3 to 4 cloves garlic (crushed)
1 large bell pepper (chopped)
1 carrot (unpeeled – scrubbed and diced)
1 large red potato (unpeeled and diced)
28-ounce can organic diced fire roasted tomatoes (do not drain)
2 Jalapeño peppers (seeded and diced)
2 15-ounce cans organic pinto beans (do not drain)
2½ cups water
2 tablespoons Better Than Bouillon Vegetable Base
1 teaspoon ground cumin

3 teaspoons fresh basil (chopped)
¼ teaspoon dried oregano
2 teaspoons fresh lime juice
1 heaping tablespoon chili powder
1 to 3 teaspoons Tabasco Sauce (depending on how hot you like it)
1 teaspoon salt

Directions:
Plug in your slow cooker and set the heat to high.

Add oil, onions and garlic to a large skillet and sauté over medium heat for about five minutes. Add bell pepper, carrot, potato, tomatoes (including liquid) and Jalapeño peppers. Deglaze pan and cook for another five minutes.

Add beans (including liquid) and water to slow cooker. Add onion mixture and next seven ingredients (bouillon to Tabasco Sauce) to slow cooker. Cover and cook for four hours. Taste and adjust for salt if necessary. Cover and refrigerate.

To reheat, cook in a large soup pot over medium heat for 15 minutes or until bubbly hot.

33 Hearty Ratatouille *VEGAN*

Ratatouille can be described as a vegetable stew. This Ratatouille is a *hearty* and thick vegan vegetable stew. Classic Ratatouille includes eggplant, zucchini, tomatoes, red onions and herbs. This recipe is different in that it includes all of the classic ingredients *plus* fennel, bay leaves, and harissa (to give it a kick).

I've also included kidney beans for extra protein. Serve with quinoa or rice on the side and a hunk of fresh bread for a complete meal.

Ingredients:
3 tablespoons extra-virgin olive oil
2 small red onions (quartered and sliced thin)
1 yellow bell pepper (cut into thin 1½-inch strips)
1 red bell pepper (cut into thin 1½-inch strips)
1 large fennel bulb (trim and slice thin)
3 garlic cloves (minced)
2 medium zucchini (washed and cut into ½-inch rounds)
1 medium eggplant (peeled and cut into ½-inch dice)
28-ounce can diced tomatoes
4 sprigs fresh thyme
4 sprigs fresh oregano
2 bay leaves
½ teaspoon gluten-free harissa paste
1 cup water
15-ounce can kidney beans (rinsed and drained)
Salt and pepper to taste
Zest of 1 lemon

Directions:

Heat oil in large saucepan or Dutch oven over medium heat. Add onions, bell peppers, and fennel, and sauté five to seven minutes, or until vegetables are translucent. Stir in garlic, then zucchini, eggplant, tomatoes, thyme, oregano, bay leaves, harissa paste, and water. If you like it spicy, use at least one teaspoon of harissa. Cover, reduce heat to medium-low, and simmer for 25 minutes.

Add kidney beans, cover, and cook for 15 minutes more. Add salt and pepper to taste, cover and refrigerate.

To serve, reheat in a large saucepan over medium heat for 15 to 20 minutes or until heated through. Garnish with lemon zest before serving.

34 Jalapeño Cheese Bread

I had a jones for jalapeño cheese bread the other morning and was too lazy to make a yeast-bread so I created this quick-bread version. I think you'll like.

In addition to toasting and enjoying it with my coffee in the morning, I like to cut it into strips and serve it with a fresh garden salad at dinnertime.

Ingredients
1 cup extra-sharp cheddar cheese (grated)
½ cup extra-sharp cheddar cheese (cut into quarter-inch cubes)
½ cup pepitas (toasted)
1 tablespoon fresh sage (minced)
½ cup nacho Jalapeño slices
1¾ cups flour
1 tablespoon baking powder
½ teaspoon salt
¼ teaspoon fresh ground black pepper
3 large eggs
1/3 cup whole milk
1/3 cup extra-virgin olive oil

Directions:
Preheat oven to 350 degrees. Generously grease an 8x4-inch loaf pan. Set aside.

Combine cheese, pepitas, sage and jalapeños in mixing bowl. Stir in flour, baking powder, salt, and pepper. Set aside.

In another mixing bowl, whisk together eggs, milk, and olive oil. Pour egg mixture over cheese/flour mixture and stir just until dry ingredients are moistened (dough will be very sticky). Transfer dough to prepared loaf pan. Spread dough evenly throughout pan.

Bake bread until golden on top and slender knife inserted into center of bread comes out clean; about 55 minutes. Remove from oven and cool bread in pan for five minutes, then turn out onto rack and cool completely.

When cool, wrap in plastic wrap and refrigerate or freeze until ready to slice and serve!

35 Idaho Potatoes

My friend, Frances, sent this recipe from her home in Idaho. It is written on a 3x5 inch index card and has a small lapel pin attached to the card. The pin is in the shape of a potato. The recipe was handed down to Frances from her mom and is approximately 90 years old.

What was good then, is certainly good now if not even better. Be sure to use Idaho potatoes and your choice of cornflakes. Both of these ingredients make a difference in the casserole's taste.

Ingredients:
8 medium Russet potatoes
1 bay leaf
1 can cream of celery soup (the original recipe calls for cream of chicken)
1½ cups sour cream
½ teaspoon salt
¼ teaspoon pepper
3 green onions (sliced)
2 cups cheddar cheese (grated)
½ cup corn flakes

Directions:
Preheat oven to 350 degrees.

Cook potatoes (boil in skins) with a bay leaf until barely tender. It is important not to overcook the potatoes or the consistency will be mushy. Remove bay leaf from potatoes. Cool potatoes, peel and grate coarsely (or use a ricer if you have one). Mix soup, sour cream, salt, pepper, green onions and 1½ cups of the cheese. Pour this mixture over potatoes and stir gently until just blended. Spoon into a greased 2½ quart casserole dish. Bake uncovered for 30 minutes. Remove from oven.

Combine remaining cheese with cornflakes and sprinkle over casserole. Bake, uncovered, for another 10 to 15 minutes. Remove from oven and allow to cool before covering and refrigerating.

To reheat, set oven to 325 degrees. Bake uncovered for 20 minutes or until heated through.

36 Jalapeño Corn Chowder

What's the difference between soup and chowder? Chowders are usually thicker and sometimes creamy. Soups are usually lighter and thinner.

Our son, Robert, and I love spicy food. Always looking for something new, we created this quick and simple soup one cold winter day last year. Fresh roasted peppers is ideal but buying them in the bottle at your favorite market works too, and keeps the prep time to less than five minutes total. To make it a true "chowder" consider breaking up soda crackers and adding them to your bowl as you sit and chow down.

Ingredients:
3 cups frozen whole kernel corn
1 14-ounce can vegetable broth
¼ cup roasted red peppers (sliced thin)
1 Jalapeño pepper (seeded and chopped)
1 cup half and half
¾ cup Cotija cheese (for garnish)
¼ cup fresh cilantro (chopped – for garnish)

Directions:
In a blender, combine half of the corn and half of the broth. Cover and blend until fairly smooth. Pour into a large soup pan. Add the balance of the corn, broth and the peppers. Bring to a boil and reduce to simmer. Stir in half and half and simmer for 20 minutes to allow flavors to develop. Be careful not to let it boil after adding the half and half. Cover and refrigerate.

To serve, reheat in a large saucepan over medium heat for about 15 minutes or until heated through. Sprinkle each serving of soup with Cotija cheese and cilantro.

37   Jim's Mom's Southern Candied Yams

When Robin and I were quite young, we were adopted into a large Greek family. We celebrated Thanksgiving and Christmas with them for over 30 years. One of the members of the family was a country boy from Georgia, Jim White, who made wonderful candied yams as his contribution to their Christmas dinners.

I asked Jim where he got the inspiration for his yam dish. He said, "My mom used to make them. After she passed away, I've made these each Christmas in her memory. I hope you enjoy them." I asked Jim what the secret was to his mom's recipe. He replied, "A generous amount of southern-distilled bourbon."

Jim passed away before I could get his recipe. But with a little effort (and a generous amount of bourbon), I re-created Jim's mom's wonderful dish. I've made my version of his recipe for our Christmas dinners ever since. My hope is that you will enjoy them as much as we do.

Ingredients:
3 medium garnet yams
8 tablespoons butter
½ cup crushed pineapple
1 teaspoon ground cinnamon
½ teaspoon ground nutmeg
¼ teaspoon ground clove
¼ teaspoon ground ginger
1 cup cane sugar
¼ cup brown sugar

2 ounces bourbon (I like *Lazy Guy Side Track Bourbon*)
¼ cup walnuts (chopped)

Directions:
Preheat the oven to 350 degrees. Prepare a 9x9-inch baking dish with cooking spray.

Peel and cut yams into ¼-inch slices. Parboil in a large saucepan over high heat for five minutes. Drain, and rinse with cold water (to stop the cooking process). Set aside.

Place the butter into a medium saucepan and melt over medium heat. Add pineapple, cinnamon, nutmeg, clove, ginger, and sugars. Remove from heat and mix thoroughly.

Overlap half of the yam slices in baking dish. Evenly sprinkle half the walnuts on top. Pour half of the butter mixture on top of this layer. Overlap the balance of the yams on top that. Pour in the balance of the butter mixture and spread it evenly over the top. Pour all of the bourbon over the top of this and sprinkle with the balance of the walnuts.

Cover with foil and bake for 40 minutes. Allow to cool and then cover and refrigerate.

To reheat, set oven to 325 degrees. Bake, uncovered, for 20 minutes or until heated through.

38 Kale-Wakame Soup *VEGAN*

A friend asked me the other day, "What can I do with all this kale growing in my garden?" I wanted to answer *Well, why not eat it?* but decided he had had enough of my obnoxious behavior recently. Instead I answered, "You won't believe this but I have a wonderful vegan recipe that combines fresh kale with edible seaweed. I think you'd love it." He looked at me like I was crazy. "I don't do seaweed," he replied.

I sent my friend this recipe. He made it for dinner and was pleasantly surprised. If you have not experienced this kale-wakame combination, give it a try. You, like my friend, will love it.

Ingredients:
¼ cup wakame
1 tablespoon extra-virgin olive oil
1 stalk celery (diced)
1 small yellow onion (diced)
2 small carrots (diced)
15-oz. can cannellini beans (rinsed and drained)
1½ cups baby lima beans
6 cups vegetable broth
1 tablespoon Better Than Bouillon Vegetable Base
1 bunch fresh kale (ribs trimmed off)
¼ teaspoon dried oregano
1/8 teaspoon ground nutmeg
1/8 teaspoon cayenne pepper

Directions:

Place wakame in small bowl. Cover with cold water and soak 15 minutes or until soft. Drain, squeeze out liquid, and set aside.

Heat oil in a large saucepan over medium heat. Add celery, onion and carrots. Sauté for about five minutes, or until tender. Add beans, broth and vegetable base. Bring to a boil, reduce heat to medium-low and simmer, covered, 10 minutes. Role kale leaves up and slice into ribbons. Add kale to the pan. Cook five minutes more, or until kale is tender. Stir in oregano, nutmeg, cayenne, and wakame. Cover and refrigerate.

To reheat, place soup in a large saucepan and reheat over medium heat for 15 minutes or until heated through.

Tip: For a heartier soup, add eight ounces of firm organic tofu (cut into 1-inch cubes) at the same time you add the beans, broth and vegetable base.

39 Kohlrabi Soup

Kohlrabi is a crispy, crunchy alien looking vegetable that you can prepare in more ways than you ever thought possible. Don't be put off by its appearance even if it does look like someone teleported a Martian vegetable right into your kitchen. Think of it as a cousin to Brussels sprouts, kale and cabbage (which it is). My favorite way to enjoy fresh, farm grown kohlrabi is in this simple soup.

Ingredients:
1 pound kohlrabi
1 medium onion (chopped)
2 stalks celery (sliced)
2 tablespoons butter
2 ½ cups vegetable broth
2 ½ cups whole milk
1 bay leaf
Salt and pepper to taste

Directions:
Remove the leaves from the kohlrabi bulbs. Peel the bulbs making sure to remove any woody parts as well as the tough green skin. Chop into 1-inch cubes. Select the most tender kohlrabi leaves and slice them in thin ¼-inch ribbons.

Place the onion in a stockpot with the butter. Sauté on medium-high heat for five minutes. Add the celery, kohlrabi cubes and ribbons of leaf. Sauté for three minutes more. Add the broth, milk and bay leaf. Bring to a boil. Reduce heat to simmer and cover. Cook for 25 to 30 minutes or until kohlrabi cubes are tender. Add salt and pepper to taste and be sure to remove the bay leaf. Cover and refrigerate.

To serve, place soup in large saucepan and reheat on medium heat for 20 minutes or until soup is heated through.

40   Mac 'N' Cheese with Smoked Gouda

Research on the internet shows that Gouda, is a Dutch cheese named after the city of Gouda in the Netherlands. It is said to be one of the most popular cheeses in the world, accounting for 50 to 60 percent of the world's cheese consumption. Smoked Gouda is a variant of this famous cheese and is smoked in ancient brick ovens over flaming hickory chip embers. Sensational with beer, this hard cheese has an edible, brown rind and a creamy, yellow interior. It is great in sandwiches and burgers.

What the internet fails to mention is that smoked Gouda is gooda in Mac N Cheese. OK. Bad play on words. But trust me when I say it really does make the best Mac & Cheese. This is the perfect comfort food for anytime, anywhere. I say, "Go for it!"

Ingredients:
12 ounces Fusilli pasta
1 tablespoon unsalted butter
2½ cups heavy cream
¼ teaspoon freshly ground white pepper
4 to 5 ounces smoked Gouda cheese (grated including the rind)
Parsley (for garnish)

Directions:
Preheat the oven to 375 degrees.

Cook Fusilli according to package directions. Drain and set aside.

In a wide, heavy pan with lots of surface area, heat butter over medium heat. Slowly add the cream and whisk to combine. Add white pepper and whisk to incorporate. Let simmer on medium low heat for about 20 minutes, stirring occasionally, without cover to reduce.

Remove the white sauce from the heat and stir in cheese. Continue stirring until the cheese melts.

Combine the cheese sauce and macaroni in a large mixing bowl and mix well. Pour into a lightly greased casserole dish, cover, and bake for 20 minutes. Remove and allow to cool before covering and refrigerating.

To serve, bake covered for 20 minutes at 350 degrees or until heated through. Remove cover from dish and switch oven to broil mode. Broil for two minutes or until lightly browned on top.

41 Matzo Ball Soup

I always thought matzo ball soup was just flour dumplings in chicken soup. As a vegetarian I never tried it. I didn't understand that it is truly comfort food so for 50 years I avoided it not thinking to look for a vegetarian version.

While in Von's the other day I found myself looking at various foodstuffs including a package of Manischewitz "Matzo Ball & Soup Mix". I decided to see what ingredients went into the soup. Before I even got to the ingredients I saw a label that read, "This product is lactose free and vegetarian". Reading the ingredients supported their claim. "Maybe" I said, "it's time to see what all the hoopla is about". I purchased the soup mix, jumped in the car and probably went too fast through downtown Ojai.

When I got home I made the balls and the soup per instructions and waited 20 minutes for it to cook. When the timer went off I lifted the lid on the soup pan and was greeted with a wonderful aroma. The site of the matzo balls floating on top was welcoming. I knew, at that moment, that I was gonna like it.

So I thought "There's got to be a recipe out there for vegetarians". And sure enough there was but I wanted to try to make it myself. So I turned to the Internet for an introductory course on basic matzo balls.

I now know what matzo meal is about and where to buy it. I'm told you can substitute cracker crumbs for matzo meal. That sounds reasonable but somehow it just doesn't sound right. I did substitute vegetable broth for chicken stock, which for a vegetarian, sounds spot on. There also seems to be a debate about whether the matzo balls should be floaters or sinkers. My recipe appeals to floater enthusiasts!

I added herbs as found on the Manischewitz box (but not the garlic, MSG or the monocalcium phosphate – whatever that is) and experimented until I got just the right mix of everything. It took three tries!

Then, before you could say l'chayim, I had a wonderful vegetarian version cooking under a tight lid on my stove. Even though it is made without schmaltz, matzo ball soup is comfort food for sure.

Ingredients:
2 tablespoons vegetable oil
2 eggs (slightly beaten)
2 tablespoons water (ice cold)
½ cup matzo meal
¼ teaspoon salt
¼ teaspoon pepper
6 cups vegetable broth
1 teaspoon Better Than Bouillon (vegetable base)
1 teaspoon fresh dill (chopped fine)
1 small carrot (grated)
Fresh flat leaf parsley (for garnish)

Directions:

Place first six ingredients in a large mixing bowl. Mix well. After mixing cover and refrigerate for one hour.

Fill a large pot with the broth, bouillon, dill and grated carrot. Bring to a boil. After it boils, reduce to a simmer.

Take the matzo mixture out of the refrigerator and gently make 1-inch balls by hand (be sure to wet your hands before forming balls). Slowly add the balls to the hot broth. Cover and cook on low for about 30 minutes.

Do not remove the lid during cooking! After cooking, turn off heat and remove cover. Let stand for at least five minutes before covering and refrigerating.

To serve, reheat soup in a large saucepan over medium heat for about 15 minutes or until balls are heated through. Garnish with parsley if desired.

42 Mushroom Goulash *VEGAN*

The origins of goulash have been traced to the 9th century, to stews eaten by Magyar (Hungarian) shepherds. Before setting out with their flocks, the shepherds prepared a portable stock of food by slowly cooking cut-up meats with onions and other flavorings until the liquids had been absorbed. This stew was then dried in the sun and packed into bags made of sheep's stomachs. At mealtime, water was added to a portion of the meat to reconstitute it, and the stew heated to taste.

This vegan recipe was inspired by a goulash recipe found in Food and Wine Magazine. It features two types of mushrooms, onions, Yukon Gold potatoes, Hungarian peppers and sweet Hungarian paprika. If you can't find Hungarian wax peppers, substitute banana wax peppers and add a teaspoon of cayenne pepper to the stew.

Ingredients:
¼ cup extra-virgin olive oil
2 yellow onions (chopped)
12 ounces Hungarian wax peppers (cored, seeded and chopped)
1½ pounds Shitake mushrooms (cleaned and cut into 1-inch pieces)
1½ pounds Cremini mushrooms (cleaned and quartered)
Salt and fresh ground pepper to taste
4 garlic cloves (minced)
1 teaspoon caraway seeds (crushed)
6 tablespoons sweet Hungarian paprika

28-ounce can diced tomatoes
2 medium Yukon Gold potatoes (peeled and cut into 1-inch pieces)
3 small saucer squash (cut into 1-inch pieces)
6 cups vegetable broth
2 bay leaves
2 tablespoons fresh breadcrumbs
Chopped parsley (for garnish)

Directions:
Heat the oil in a large pot over medium heat. Add the onions and peppers and cook for about six minutes. Add the mushrooms, season with salt and pepper, and cook on medium-high heat until for about eight to 10 minutes or until reduced and browned.

Add the garlic and caraway seeds to the pot. Stir in paprika, tomatoes, potatoes and squash. Add the broth and bay leaves, season with salt and pepper (if needed), and bring to a boil. Cover and cook over low heat for about an hour, stirring once or twice.

Add breadcrumbs and cook until slightly thickened. To serve, ladle goulash into bowls and garnish with a sprinkle of chopped parsley.

Tip: If you are a lacto-ovo vegetarian, you might also enjoy a dollop of sour cream on top!

43 Portobello Wellington Appetizers

Are you looking for an amazing appetizer to add to your New Year's celebration table? Look no further.

The pairing of Portobello mushroom earthiness with fresh winter kale and the creamy goodness of Stilton cheese will delight both family and friends. Serve with a sparkling wine and this is a combination that can't be beat.

Here's an added bonus: these puff pastry appetizers can be made ahead of time and kept refrigerated until ready to bake.

Ingredients:
4 medium Portobello mushrooms
4 tablespoons extra-virgin olive oil
1 bunch fresh red chard (ribs trimmed, leaves cut into ribbons)
1 clove garlic (minced)
1 teaspoon fresh lemon juice
Salt and pepper to taste
4 ounces Stilton cheese (sliced)
1 package puff pastry sheets
1 large egg (beaten)
1 tablespoon fresh thyme leaves

Directions:
Preheat oven to 400 degrees.

Remove the stalks from the mushrooms and brush off the tops. Heat two tablespoons of the oil in a large frying pan on medium heat and cook for three to four minutes on each side until golden and cooked through. Remove the mushrooms from the pan and set the pan and the mushrooms aside.

Clean chard leaves under running cold water. Hold the stem of one leaf in your hand and grasping the leafy part with your other hand, tear the rib away from the stem. Discard stems and cut leaves into ¼-inch ribbons.

Place the pan back on the stove and add the other two tablespoons oil. Add the garlic and cook on medium-high heat for one minute. Add the chard to the pan, and then cook for two minutes. Remove from heat, add lemon, and season with salt and pepper to taste. Set aside.

Roll the pastry out to ⅛-inch thickness. Cut out eight circles about four inches in diameter (depending upon the size of the mushrooms). Place four pastry circles on a baking tray lined with parchment paper.

Top each circle with a quarter of the chard. Top the chard with a slice of cheese, then a mushroom, smooth-side up, and top the mushroom with another slice of cheese. Brush the border to each circle with egg, then gently stretch one of the four remaining circles over the cheese and press the edges together with a fork. Repeat three more times.

Brush the tops with egg wash and sprinkle thyme leaves on top. Bake for 25 to 30 minutes or until golden. Remove from oven and cool on a rack for five minutes before wrapping and refrigerating.

To reheat, place on a baking sheet an oven set to 350 degrees. Bake for 10 minutes or until heated through. Serve with a side of gravy if desired.

44 Roasted Red Pepper and Carrot Soup *VEGAN*

This is a popular vegan soup if for no other reason than it is easy to make and goes from the stove to the table in 60 minutes. In addition, the carrots and bell peppers have beta-carotene, which is a good source of anti-oxidants.

The combination of carrots and red bell peppers provides a beautiful color to this soup and, with the *roasted* peppers, a full-bodied flavor. The addition of lemon juice just before serving is a nice flavor flash that enhances the flavor of the roasted peppers.

Here is my take on this smooth-textured, richly flavored soup. For a complete meal, serve with a loaf of fresh-baked bread.

Ingredients:
2 large red bell peppers
2 tablespoons olive oil
½ teaspoon curry powder
1 large bay leaf
1 large onion (sliced)
2 large carrots (sliced)
4 cloves garlic (sliced thin)
1 teaspoon salt
4 cups low sodium vegetable broth
2 tablespoons fresh lemon juice

Directions:

Place bell peppers on baking sheet, place on the middle rack of the oven and set a timer for seven minutes. Broil on one side until the timer goes off or the skin is black and blistery. Remove from the oven, turn them "one quarter" to expose an un-blistered side, set the timer for seven minutes, and broil until the timer goes off. Do this for all four sides. Remove the peppers from the oven and place in a large closeable baggie. When peppers are cool enough to handle, remove from the bag and rub off the blackened peel. Remove seeds. Set aside.

While the peppers are roasting, heat oil in saucepan over medium heat. Add curry powder and bay leaf and stir to combine. Add onions, carrots, garlic, and salt. Continue cooking for 8 minutes more or until onion is translucent. Add broth and bring to a boil. Cover and reduce heat to medium-low. Simmer for 25 minutes.

Remove bay leaf and transfer carrot mixture to blender. Add bell peppers and purée until smooth. Stir in lemon juice. Cover and refrigerate.

To serve, reheat soup in a large saucepan over medium heat for 15 minutes or until heated through. Transfer soup to four bowls and serve while still hot.

45   Robin's Tortilla Soup

This is a wonderful, flavorful soup that is easy to prepare. Robin first made it in our home in Ojai and as it was simmering on the stove, the aroma made me smile. Make this soup and serve with fresh, warm tortillas or bolillo bread. Leave out the cheese and this is totally vegan!

Ingredients:
2 cups green snap beans (cut into 1-inch lengths)
2 cloves garlic (minced)
2 small zucchini (cubed)
1 medium potato (diced)
1 cup tomatillos (chopped)
14-ounce can diced tomatoes (Mexican-style is good)
1 medium onion (chopped)
1 medium bell pepper (chopped)
1 tablespoon chipotle peppers in adobo sauce (use the sauce - not the peppers)
½ teaspoon cumin
½ teaspoon oregano
6 cups vegetable broth
½ teaspoon salt
2 tablespoons fresh lime juice
½ cup fresh cilantro (chopped)
1 cup Cotija Queso Seco (crumbled for garnish)
Tortilla strips (lightly salted corn tortilla strips)

Directions:

Using a large pot, combine beans, garlic, zucchini, potato, tomatillos, tomatoes, onion, bell pepper, adobo sauce, cumin, oregano and vegetable broth. Bring to a boil. Reduce heat, cover and simmer for 20 minutes or more. Remove from heat. Allow to cool and then refrigerate.

To reheat, put soup in a large pot. Reheat on medium heat for about 15 minutes or until soup begins to bubble around the sides. Then stir in salt, lime juice and cilantro. Ladle soup into individual bowls and garnish with Cotija cheese and tortilla strips just prior to serving.

46 Spicy Cauliflower Garbanzo Coconut Stew

This vegan and gluten-free dish is the perfect hot meal for a cold, blustery late-winter supper. Cauliflower and garbanzo beans (chickpeas) are the perfect complement to the Indian spices and the unsweetened coconut is a welcome addition.

Ingredients :
¼ teaspoon red pepper flakes
1 teaspoon ground cumin
½ teaspoon ground cardamom
½ teaspoon black pepper
2 teaspoons garam masala
½ teaspoon smoked paprika
1 tablespoon coconut oil
3 cloves garlic (minced)
5 Roma tomatoes (sliced into 1-inch chunks)
1 onion (chopped)
1 cup carrots (chopped)
⅓ cup unsweetened coconut flakes
2 teaspoon sea salt
⅓ cup water
2 cups fresh cauliflower florets
15-ounce can garbanzo beans (drained)
1 tablespoon lime juice
Salt to taste
1 tablespoon fresh mint (chopped for garnish)

Directions:
Combine the first six ingredients (pepper flakes through paprika) in a small prep bowl and set this spice mixture aside.

Heat coconut oil in a large pot over medium heat. Add spice mixture and stir to combine. Cook spices for about 60 seconds and then add garlic, tomatoes, onions, carrots, and coconut. Sauté for 10 minutes. Add salt and water and bring to a boil. Reduce heat to medium and cook, covered, for another 20 minutes, or until vegetables are tender.

Transfer all of the cooked vegetables to blender or food processor and puree until smooth. Return all of vegetable mixture (blended or not) to pot.

Add cauliflower, garbanzo beans, and lemon juice. Bring to a boil, reduce heat to medium and cook, covered, for 15 minutes or until cauliflower is tender. Add additional salt to taste. Cover and refrigerate.

To reheat, cook on medium heat for 15 minutes or until heated through. Transfer to a large bowl and garnish with chopped mint. Serve with a large bowl of steaming quinoa (made with vegetable broth instead of water.)

Tip: I also like to blend half of the vegetables leaving the other half un-blended for added texture. Your choice!

47 Tabouli Salad

Also spelled tabbouleh or tabouleh, tabouli is a traditional Eastern Mediterranean salad served throughout Lebanon, Syria, Jordan and Southern Turkey. The basis of Tabouli, bulgar wheat, has been around for over 4,000 years.

Bulgar is processed by steaming the whole-wheat kernels, drying them and then crushing them. This process gives the wheat a fine, nutty flavor and requires little or no cooking. Purists swear that bulgar wheat differs remarkably from cracked wheat berries. As far as taste and nutrition, either product will work well in this recipe. If you use cracked wheat it will require a little more cooking time.

Enjoy Tabouli as a side dish, an appetizer or a lettuce wrap filling. I like to serve this vegan dish on a bed of Bibb lettuce with a side of Pita bread and Hummus.

Ingredients:
1¼ cups bulgur wheat
4 cups boiling water
1½ cups fresh parsley (minced)
¾ cup fresh mint (minced)
¾ cup green onion (minced)
3 medium tomatoes (diced)
½ cup lemon juice
¼ cup extra-virgin olive oil
1 teaspoon salt
1 cup cooked chickpeas (garbanzo beans)

Directions:
Pour four cups boiling water over bulgur wheat cover and let stand for about an hour or until all liquid is absorbed. Combine bulgur with the rest of the ingredients and mix well. Cover and place in refrigerator until ready to serve.

Tip: As a change you can add half a chopped cucumber. Robin does this and it gives the salad a nice, fresh finish.

48 Tahini-Herb Dip *VEGAN*

Serve with pita chips, crackers, or raw vegetables.

Ingredients:
1 garlic clove (minced)
½ cup fresh parsley leaves
¼ cup chopped fresh chives
¼ cup tahini
¼ cup water
2 tablespoons fresh lemon juice
2 tablespoons extra-virgin olive oil
2 teaspoons agave nectar
6 cups vegetables such as broccoli florets, carrot sticks, cauliflower florets, celery sticks, cucumber slices and grape tomatoes

Directions:
In food processor, purée garlic, parsley, chives, tahini, water, lemon juice, olive oil and honey until smooth. Transfer to small bowl, cover, and refrigerate overnight for best flavor.

49   Chèvre Cheese Pasta - Mac & Cheese Style

I stumbled upon this dish at a restaurant in San Luis Obispo. Always looking for something different I began experimenting at home until I got it just right. Here's my riff on a simple Mac and Cheese with fresh Chève (goat cheese).

Creamy...tangy...different. This is not Mac & Cheese from a box!

Ingredients:
12 ounces fusilli, rotini, or rocchetti pasta
1 tablespoon unsalted butter
2 ½ cups heavy cream
¼ teaspoon freshly ground black pepper
5 ounces fresh herb Chèvre cheese
1 teaspoon lemon zest (chopped fine)
2 tablespoon panko breadcrumbs
2 tablespoons Asiago cheese (grated fine)
1 tablespoon parsley (chopped for garnish)

Directions:
Preheat the oven to 375 degrees.

Cook pasta according to package directions. Drain and set aside.

In a wide, heavy pan with lots of surface area, heat butter over medium heat. Slowly add the cream and whisk to combine. Let simmer on medium low heat for about 15 to 20 minutes, stirring occasionally, without a cover so that it reduces. Add pepper and whisk to incorporate. Remove this white sauce from the heat and stir in Chève and lemon zest. Continue stirring until the cheese melts.

Combine the cheese sauce and pasta in a large mixing bowl and mix well. Pour into a lightly greased casserole dish, cover, and bake for 20 minutes. Remove from oven and remove cover.

Mix panko breadcrumbs and Asiago cheese together. Sprinkle over pasta. Put back in oven under the broiler and broil for about two minutes or until top begins to brown. Remove from oven and allow to cool. Cover and refrigerate overnight.

To serve, place in oven set at 350 degrees and bake for 15 minutes or until heated through. Remove cover from dish and switch oven to broil mode. Broil for two minutes or until lightly browned on top. Remove from oven, sprinkle parsley on top, and serve while piping hot.

50 Tarragon Salad Dressing VEGAN

Although American cuisine does not favor tarragon, it is a major flavoring in French cuisine including béarnaise sauce and fines herbs. The French call it the "King of Herbs."

The ancient Greeks reportedly used it as a remedy for toothaches. Today, we know that tarragon contains an anesthetic chemical, eugenol, which figures prominently in anesthetic clove oil. See the movie Marathon Man for a disturbing use of clove oil as an anesthetic. On second thought, even though Dustin Hoffman is amazing in his role as Babe, skip the movie! It is disturbing.

Tarragon loses potency as it dries. This may be one reason it is frequently preserved in vinegar, which captures its essence and provides tastiness when used in salad dressings. But why purchase tarragon vinegar when you can enjoy fresh tarragon from your garden?

Here's a creamy salad dressing recipe using fresh tarragon (we also use it as a dip for steamed artichokes):

Ingredients:
½ cup Vegenaise
¼ cup salad oil
1 tablespoon lemon juice
1 tablespoon white wine vinegar
1 teaspoon Tamari sauce
¼ teaspoon pepper

1 clove garlic (minced)
1½ tablespoons fresh tarragon (minced)

Directions:
In a small bowl, whisk Vegenaise, oil, lemon juice, vinegar, soy sauce, pepper and garlic. Add tarragon and mix well. Cover and refrigerate overnight to allow tarragon's goodness to infuse the dressing.

51 Robin's Three Bean Salad ^{VEGAN}

This is Robin's recipe for three bean salad and, like most, consists of green beans and kidney beans. Unlike most, it substitutes white beans for garbanzo beans. Her dressing gives it a sweet, tangy bite that is irresistibly good.

Ingredients:
2 - 15 ounce can green beans (drained)
2 - 15 ounce can white beans (drained and rinsed)
2 - 15 ounce can kidney beans (drained and rinsed)
2½ cups red onion (chopped)
1 cup granulated sugar
1 1/3 cup red wine vinegar
2/3 cup vegetable oil
1 teaspoon salt
1 teaspoon ground black pepper
1 teaspoon celery seed
1 teaspoon dried tarragon
Salt and ground black pepper to taste

Directions:
Gently mix all ingredients together. Cover and refrigerate for at least 3 hours before serving.

52 Forbidden Rice *VEGAN*

Forbidden Rice gets its name from a Chinese legend that says it was only grown for consumption by Emperors and not to be consumed by the general population. Don't know if the legend is true, but it is interesting. The rice is also interesting.

Unlike the familiar California long grain rice we usually see on our dinner plates, this is a short, black rice. The black color is attributed to high amounts of melanin in the bran. When you cook it, Forbidden Rice turns a dark purple and has a nutty taste and aroma similar to wild rice.

When pomegranates are in season I add them to this recipe. Buy one and use the colorful seeds as garnish for this sweet-hot Forbidden Rice salad side dish.

Ingredients:
2 cups Forbidden Rice
4 cups water
½ cup agave nectar (room temperature)
½ cup red wine vinegar
2 tablespoons Tamari sauce
1½ teaspoons salt
1 teaspoon sesame oil
½ teaspoon cayenne pepper
½ teaspoon freshly ground black pepper
1 tablespoon dry sherry
1/8 teaspoon ground cloves
½ cup vegetable oil
¾ cup grated carrots

1 yellow bell pepper (seeded and diced)
1 cup cucumber (thinly sliced)
¾ cup roasted pecans (chopped)
½ cup thinly sliced green onions
Pomegranate seeds (garnish)

Directions:
Place rice and water in a medium pot, cover with a tight-fitting lid, bring quickly to a boil, then reduce heat and simmer. Don't peek. Cook for 50 minutes. Stir cooked rice to break up clumps, then set aside to cool in a large bowl. Cover and refrigerate.

Make the dressing by whisking together the next nine ingredients (agave through cloves), then drizzle in the oil, stirring constantly to blend. Combine the carrots, bell pepper, cucumber and half of the dressing in a medium bowl. Cover rice and refrigerate. Cover and refrigerate the balance of the dressing.

Just before serving, add the carrot mixture to the rice and stir gently, adding more of the extra dressing as needed. Mix in toasted pecans and green onions and serve on chilled salad plates.

Index of Recipes by Title

Asparagus and Gruyère Quiche (21)
Back-to-Our Root Vegetables (22)
Black Beans, Chard and Sorghum Bowl (13)
Bread Pudding (18)
Brown Rice & Black Bean Casserole (3)
Burrata Lasagna (23)
Cabbage and Chickpea Soup (24) *VEGAN*
Chana Masala (25) *VEGAN*
Cheesy-Creamy Cauliflower (26)
Chève Cheese Pasta - Mac & Cheese Style (49)
Chickpea Veggie Patty Burger (27)
Chik'n Enchiladas (5)
Collard Greens with Veggie Sausage (28)
Creamy Vodka Sauce (29)
Earthy Mushroom & Gruyère Quiche (30)
Eggplant Parmigiano-Reggiano (4)
Forbidden Rice Salad (52) *VEGAN*
Gran's Carrot Casserole (31)
Hearty Cannellini Bean Casserole (6) *VEGAN*
Hearty Chili Bean Soup (32) *VEGAN*
Hearty Kale & Sausage Turnovers (7)
Hearty Quinoa Burger (8)
Hearty Ratatouille (33) *VEGAN*
Idaho Potatoes (35)
Jalapeño Cheese Bread (34)
Jalapeño Corn Chowder (36)
Jim's Mom's Southern Candied Yams (37)
Jollof Rice Bowl (9)
Kale-Wakame Soup (38) *VEGAN*
Kohlrabi Soup (39)
Lemony Artichoke Turnovers (10)

Mac 'N' Cheese with Smoked Gouda (40)
Malt Ball Cupcakes (11)
Marinara Sauce (12) *VEGAN*
Matzo Ball Soup (41)
Meaty Nut Loaf (1)
Mushroom Goulash (42) *VEGAN*
Oatmeal Bread (14)
Orzo Pasta with Asiago Cheese (15)
Portobello Wellington Appetizers (43)
Quinoa and Chik'n Casserole (16) *VEGAN*
Roasted Red Pepper and Carrot Soup (44) *VEGAN*
Robin's Tortilla Soup (45)
Robin's Three Bean Salad (51) *VEGAN*
Spicy Cauliflower Garbanzo Coconut Stew (46)
Tabouli Salad (47)
Tahini-Herb Dip (48) *VEGAN*
Tarragon Salad Dressing (50) *VEGAN*
Tempeh Salisbury Steak (17)
Three Cheese Lasagna (2)
Vegetarian Jambalaya (19)
Veggie Meatballs (20)

Index of Ingredients by Recipe

agave nectar, 49, 52
Aleppo pepper, 9
almonds, 1
apples, 7, 18
artichoke, 10
Asiago cheese, 15, 49
asparagus, 21
avocados, 8, 13
baking powder, 34
baking soda, 11, 14
basil, 4, 15, 19, 33
basmati rice, 9
bay leaf, 13, 25, 33, 35, 40, 43, 44
bell pepper, 9, 19, 32, 33, 44, 45, 52
black beans, 3, 5, 13, 16
bourbon, 38
bread, 17, 18
breadcrumbs, 4, 6, 23, 26, 27, 43, 49
broccoli, 49
brown rice, 1, 3
brown sugar, 14, 37
bulgur wheat, 47
Burrata cheese, 23
butter, 5, 7, 10, 11, 15, 18, 20, 21, 23, 26, 30, 31, 37, 40
buttermilk, 11
cabbage, 24
Cajun seasoning, 19
cannellini beans, 6, 19, 38
caraway seeds, 42
cardamom, 46

carrots, 3, 6, 8, 13, 22, 31, 38, 41, 44, 46, 49, 52
cashews, 1
cauliflower, 26, 46, 49
cayenne pepper, 10, 19, 26, 38, 52
celery, 13, 19, 38, 40, 49
celery seed, 52
Chanterelle mushrooms, 23
chard, 43
Cheddar cheese, 26, 34, 35
Chevre cheese, 49
chickpeas, 24, 25, 27, 46, 47
chile pepper, 28
chili powder, 5, 16, 33
chipotle peppers, 45
chives, 49
cilantro, 35, 8, 13, 16, 25, 27, 36, 45
cinnamon, 14, 18, 25, 37
cloves, 13, 37, 52
cocoa powder, 11
coconut flakes, 46
coconut oil, 13, 25, 46
collard greens, 28
coriander, 16, 25
corn, 5, 16, 36
corn flakes, 35
cornstarch, 17, 18
Cotija cheese, 36, 45
cottage cheese, 1
cracker crumbs, 20
crackers, 31
cream, 18, 23, 26, 30, 40, 49
Cremini mushrooms, 23, 30
cucumber, 49, 52

cumin, 3, 16, 25, 32, 45, 46
curry powder, 44
dill, 41
eggplant, 4, 33
eggs, 1, 4, 11, 14, 17, 18, 20, 21, 27, 30, 31, 34, 41, 43
egg whites, 8, 30
Emmentaler cheese, 27
enchilada sauce, 16
epazote, 13
fennel, 33
flaxseed meal, 30
flour, 4, 7, 10, 11, 14, 21, 26, 30, 31, 34
Fontina cheese, 23
Forbidden Rice, 52
Fusilli pasta, 40, 49
garam masala, 25, 46
garlic, 1, 2, 4, 5, 6, 9, 10, 13, 16, 17, 19, 20, 24, 25, 26, 28, 30, 32, 33, 42, 43, 44, 45, 46, 49, 51
garlic powder, 19, 20
ginger, 9, 25, 37
Gouda cheese, 40
green beans, 52
green chiles, 3
green onions, 52
Gruyère cheese, 1, 21, 30
Habanero pepper, 9
half and half, 21, 36
harissa, 33
Hungarian peppers, 42
Jalapeño peppers, 13, 16, 32, 36
Jalapeño slices, 34
Kaiser rolls, 8

kale, 7, 38
kidney beans, 8, 33, 52
kohlrabi, 40
lasagna noodles, 2, 23
leek, 21
lemon, 27, 33
lemon juice, 43, 44, 47, 49, 50
lemon zest, 10, 49
lettuce, 8
Lightlife Italian Smart Sausages, 7, 9, 19, 28
lima beans, 38
lime juice, 13, 33, 45, 46
Longhorn cheese, 20
malted milk balls, 12
malted milk powder, 12
marjoram, 1, 23
matzo meal, 41
Mexican blend cheese, 16
milk, 10, 17, 18, 30, 34, 40
mint, 46, 47
molasses, 18
mozzarella cheese, 2, 4
mushrooms, 3
mustard, 8, 10, 30
nutmeg, 14, 18, 21, 30, 37, 38
nutritional yeast, 26
oats, 14
olive oil, 2, 3, 4, 5, 6, 9, 13, 17, 19, 22, 23, 24, 27, 28, 30, 32, 33, 34, 38, 42, 43, 44, 47, 49
onion, 2, 3, 5, 6, 7, 8, 9, 13, 13, 16, 17, 19, 20, 24, 25, 27, 28, 30, 31, 32,

33, 35, 38, 40, 42, 44, 45, 46, 47, 52
onion powder, 19
oregano, 19, 33, 33, 38, 45
orzo pasta, 15
paprika, 9, 19, 24, 42, 46
Parmesan cheese, 10, 23
Parmigiano-Reggiano cheese, 2, 4
parsley, 1, 6, 17, 20, 23, 24, 40, 41, 43, 47, 49
parsnips, 22
pecans, 52
Pecorino Romano cheese, 10
pepitas, 34
pineapple, 37
pinto beans, 32
Pomegranate seeds, 52
Portobello mushrooms, 43
potatoes, 22, 24, 32, 35, 43, 45
powdered sugar, 12
Provolone cheese, 2
puff pastry, 10, 43
Queso Cotija cheese, 8
Queso Fresco cheese, 13
quinoa, 8, 16
Quorn Vegan Chik'n Tenders, 5, 16
raisins, 7, 18
red beans, 19
red chile peppers, 25, 36
red pepper flakes, 4, 30, 46
rice, 19
ricotta cheese, 23
rocchetti pasta, 49
rotini pasta, 49

rutabaga, 22
sage, 1, 20, 34
saucer squash, 43
Serrano chile, 3
sesame oil, 52
shallot, 8, 10, 23
Shitake mushrooms, 42
snap beans, 45
sorghum, 13
sour cream, 20, 35, 43
spinach, 2, 5
sprouts, 27
Stilton cheese, 43
sun dried tomato, 2
Swiss chard, 13
Swiss cheese, 3
Tabasco sauce, 33
tahini, 49
Tamari sauce, 50, 52
tarragon, 51, 52
tempeh, 17
thyme, 1, 6, 9, 10, 19, 28, 30, 33, 43
tomatillos, 45
tomato paste, 2, 9
tomato sauce, 19, 28
tomatoes, 2, 4, 5, 9, 13, 16, 19, 24, 25, 30, 32, 33, 43, 45, 46, 47, 49
tortilla strips, 45
tortillas, 5
turmeric, 25
vanilla, 11, 18
Vegenaise, 8, 50

vegetable broth, 9, 10, 13, 15, 17, 19,
    24, 25, 28, 36, 38, 40, 41, 43, 44,
    45
vinegar, 6, 28, 50, 52, 52
vodka, 30
wakame, 38
walnuts, 1, 18, 20, 38
wheat germ, 21
whiskey, 18
white beans, 52
wine, 10, 23, 28, 52
Worcestershire (vegetarian), 17
yams, 37
zucchini squash, 3, 33, 45

About the Author

Randy has been a vegetarian since August 1975 and eats fresh and local as often as possible. He enjoys cooking for friends and family using ingredients from backyard vegetable and herb gardens. He is known locally as the "Healthy Chef" and his food is often called vegetarian comfort food. His recipe column, Chef Randy, is syndicated in coastal California newspapers. He teaches at the Ojai Culinary School.

He and his wife Robin live in Ojai, California, with their dog Willow. Robin and Willow are not vegetarians.

Ojai Valley Cookbooks: Amazon Reviews

SO, YOU'VE INHERITED A VEGETARIAN ...NOW WHAT?

"For Christmas, we gave this to a friend who "inherited" a pair of vegetarians. The title made everyone laugh, it was a huge hit!! And the recipes are easy to follow too, which is huge when you're entering this unknown territory of "vegetarian cooking." Even for someone who is a tried-and-true carnivore (me!), Randy's recipes are surprisingly REALLY tasty and satisfying. You definitely get the sense that he just loves to cook, and that he wants to share that with you. He doesn't lecture you about the evils of meat or anything, he just lays out what tastes good and what works for him. I LOVE this cookbook!"

—Logan H.

"Meat's not the only thing that sticks to your ribs. Sauces and cheeses, in my opinion, make this the tastiest of all Randy's books so far. Reading it is like having a conversation with an old friend."

—Chris L.

"As the title implies, this book is a primer for the carnivores among us who happen to have vegetarian family or friends. It also provides excellent meal ideas for meat eaters who also love excellent and creative vegetarian dishes. As with Randy's previous books, this is a book for everybody who loves good food, vegetarian or otherwise!"

—Lol S.

OJAI VALLEY VEGETARIAN COOKBOOK

"Less Paula Deen, more Randy Graham!"
—Lisa S.

"This cookbook was just what I was looking for now that our son has given up meat and fish. Now I know what to cook for him when he comes for a visit!"
—Allison W.

"Found this cookbook to be well written and full of excellent recipes and I'm not even a vegetarian! Have made the Cheese and Tomato Pie, pg 98, and will make it again, it's good hot or cold---will make the Mexican Hominy Bake next then the Leek and Potato Soup and on and on and on-------!"
—MJW

"A wonderfully tasty tome of cookery for the vegetarian who loves to show non-vegetarians just how well we eat without the meat. Entertaining stories lead into easy to follow recipes that will delight fans of "comfort" food, no matter what your tastes are. This is a great book to share with those who might be "on the fence" about vegetarianism as Chef Randy covers the range of meals and meal options, encouraging you to modify as needed. I'm confident that the Ojai Valley Vegetarian Cookbook will keep our stove warm long into the years to come. A must for any cookbook collection, vegetarian or otherwise."
—Christian

OJAI VALLEY VEGAN COOKBOOK

We didn't have Randy's new book "The Ojai Valley Vegan Cookbook", in our house more than 30 minutes before my wife, the real cook in the house, claimed it. We're not vegans or even vegetarians but this book has a bunch of "can't miss" recipes sure to please your guests no matter what camp they're in. Even if you're an accomplished griller you're going to want to read section 57 for tips on how to grill the perfect artichoke. I love the way Randy makes this book personal with family insights like section 12 where he talks about his son Robert's love of cooking and the tips that Robert passed up the family tree.

—Average Guy

This is an impressive collection of recipes, and I look forward to trying lots of them out. We believe that food is medicine and Randy encourages us all to eat local, eat well, and eat fresh. My wife and I have been mostly vegetarian since the early 70's, and we do love dairy. Yet, when I read through the 113 recipes, I know that I won't miss it at all. Thank you Randy for your commitment to offering recipes for our joy in cooking, eating and living.

—Brian B.

What a great cookbook! The recipes are easy to follow and the cookbook is so varied with so many interesting recipes to try out. I love the way he incorporates his own personal comments in every recipe that he has put in his book. I think this gives it a warmer and loving touch to it. Even if you're not vegan, everyone needs this book!

—Lynn G.

OJAI VALLEY GLUTEN-FREE COOKBOOK

"I like Randy's chatty comments before the recipes. It feels real neighborly. I have been gluten free for several years and I have really missed not eating lasagna. Randy's recipe was tasty and filling. I plan to add it to my regular rotation of favorite meals. Even my husband who prefers meat liked this recipe. Randy said it makes enough for two, I would say for four! This is much tastier and more filling than eggplant parmesan too. Next week I intend to make the Nutty Meat Loaf."

—Dianne B.

"I'm a teenager with gluten problems. This cookbook provides amazing recipes that are healthy and creative. I love to cook, and I love to eat good food with healthy ingredients, and with this book, I have access to recipes that I love!"

—MsMae

"I'm not on a gluten-free diet, but I do live a vegan lifestyle and have thoroughly enjoyed Chef Randy's previous vegetarian and vegan cookbooks. I have several friends and family members who for one reason or another require gluten-free foods and I'm super excited to test out Chef Randy's gluten-free recipes on them. What I love: The recipes are easy to follow, the stories before each recipe are heart-filled, and the ingredients required are easy to find, fresh, and good for the body and soul."

—BN11

OJAI VALLEY SLOW-COOKER COOKBOOK

Slow cooker meals are my go-to during the busy fall and winter months. I appreciate that the author provides two recipe versions, 'quicker' and 'nutritious'. The 'quicker' versions use a few short cuts, like canned or frozen vegetables but are just as satisfying. I especially like that the 'quicker' recipes use ingredients you likely have in your pantry or your freezer. I made the Butternut Squash Stew, Chili Verde and Spinach, Bean and Sausage. All were delicious and received compliments at the dinner table. The Spinach, Bean and Sausage was especially tasty and filling without being too heavy. Great variety of flavor profiles too!

—Lori H.

What a great concept! Sometimes you need to make a quick meal and sometimes you want to take more time and use fresh ingredients. This wonderful slow cook book gives you options Thank You Randy Graham for your dedication to great vegetarian meals.

—Marcia M.

Today we made the Chik'n Tikka Masala (nutritious) version and love it! The recipe was so easy to follow and the aromas filled the house quickly. The broth is nice and warn and slightly spicy. The chicken is tender and pulls apart easily and is soaked with the sauce. This will be a Fall staple in our family and I am so happy to have an easy chicken recipe to make in the future.

—Donna L.

Made in the USA
Las Vegas, NV
27 January 2021